Judy
Reamer
Daniel 4:35

How a Jewish Girl Went
From Wondering to …

WONDER

JUDY REAMER

WestBow·
PRESS
A DIVISION OF THOMAS NELSON
& ZONDERVAN

Unless otherwise noted, all Scripture quotations are from the Holy Bible, New International Version ®, NIV ® Copyright © 1973, 1978, 1984, 2011 by Biblica, Inc. ®. Used by permission. All rights reserved worldwide.

Scripture quotations marked KJV are from the King James Version of the Bible.

Scripture quotations marked CJB are from the Complete Jewish Bible by David H. Stern. Copyright © 1998. All rights reserved. Used by permission of Messianic Jewish Publishers.

WestBow Press books may be ordered through booksellers or by contacting:

WestBow Press
A Division of Thomas Nelson & Zondervan
1663 Liberty Drive
Bloomington, IN 47403
www.westbowpress.com
1 (866) 928-1240

Because of the dynamic nature of the Internet, any web addresses or links contained in this book may have changed since publication and may no longer be valid. The views expressed in this work are solely those of the author and do not necessarily reflect the views of the publisher, and the publisher hereby disclaims any responsibility for them.

Any people depicted in stock imagery provided by Thinkstock are models, and such images are being used for illustrative purposes only. Certain stock imagery © Thinkstock.

ISBN: 978-1-4908-7742-6 (sc)
ISBN: 978-1-4908-7743-3 (hc)
ISBN: 978-1-4908-7741-9 (e)

Library of Congress Control Number: 2015906344

Print information available on the last page.

WestBow Press rev. date: 4/27/2015

Dedicated to Brian, Michael, Kelly, Lauren, Stephen, Kyle, Cameron, Andrew, Ireland, August and Isabella—who each say, "I'm Grandma's favorite!" And all would be correct.

"Don't be a writer if you can get out of it! It's a solitary job, sometimes a rather lonely one (*Who's listening?* you think), and it requires relentless self-discipline. The world is not waiting with bated breath for what you turn out. A writer has to be some of kind of nut to stick with it. But if, like the psalmist, you say, 'My heart was hot within me; while I was musing the fire burned,' then perhaps you have to write."

—Elisabeth Elliot

"Amen."

—Judy Reamer

CONTENTS

PREFACE

Years ago, I read Rabbi Harold S. Kushner's popular book, *When Bad Things Happen to Good People.* His basic thesis, born out of deep personal loss and suffering, was that God is limited in his ability to deal with the problem of evil in the world. Kushner's arguments were persuasive to me and countless others; they comforted hearts like mine that were grappling with issues of pain and injustice. But I have since come to realize Kushner's comfort came at the price of disfiguring the true nature of the Almighty and sovereign God of the Universe.

The personal accounts in my story have one common theme: *How big is God!*

We are the objects of his love, and he is infinitely able to do more than anything we can imagine. While God's timing and ways may not always meet with our approval or satisfy our understanding, to me the evidence is plain and compelling: God *is* able—an idea Kushner challenged in his book. The story in the following pages refutes what the rabbi espoused.

PART ONE
THE WONDERING YEARS

*"No one knows how bad he is until he
has tried very hard to be good."*
(C. S. Lewis)

CHAPTER 1

"BECAUSE I'M JEWISH!"

Maybe you've heard of the Wandering Jew. That's not me, but I have always been a full-blown *wondering* Jew.

For two years after my parents divorced, my mother and I lived on the first floor of a four-family red-brick dwelling in Baltimore. My Russian great-grandfather Becker lived upstairs with my uncle Meyer and aunt Dot.

About the only thing Grandpa Becker and I had in common was that we were both very thin. Over and over again I heard the familiar Jewish lecture: "Eat! Eat something! You look like a string bean! Don't you know there are children in China who are starving?" I thought, *Why push me to eat? Grandpa's nearly one hundred. Being thin hasn't killed him!*

I would frequently scoot up the bare wooden stairs to the second floor, my skinny seven-year-old legs flying, to visit my aunt and uncle. I could always count on hugs and a detour through the kitchen to get some cookies—Aunt Dot's creations. I was particularly interested in her chocolate macaroons and oh! those thumbprint cookies with apricot jelly in the center.

But as strong as my sweet tooth was, my curiosity was stronger. I often wondered about my grandpa Becker. He was a mystery to me. A frail man, he stayed all day in his room wearing a yarmulke (a black cap worn by devout Jewish men), rocking back and forth in his chair, and muttering to himself.

One day I got brave enough to ask him a question. "Grandpa, what did you do in Russia?"

He was silent for a long time. Eventually he answered me.

"I owned a saloon."

After another pause, he added, "People would fight there. Sometimes they would shoot guns."

Abruptly he went back to rocking and muttering. I could tell the conversation was over. I left his room, wondering what a saloon was.

When I returned the next day for more cookies, I decided to try talking with him again.

"Grandpa, what are you doing?"

"I'm praying."

"What are you saying?"

"It's Hebrew."

"What does it mean?"

Grandpa was very quiet. Finally he said, "I don't know. I am not sure what I'm saying, but I have committed Hebrew prayers to memory."

"Well then, Grandpa, why are you doing it?"

He stared at me. Then came the answer that my "why?" questions always seemed to bring forth.

"Because I'm Jewish!"

Later that evening I asked my mother, "Why does Grandpa pray like that?" Mother explained that what Grandpa did was called *davening.* He was reciting old Hebrew prayers. They were prayers he had memorized phonetically when he was much younger. Now in his old age, people would pay him to say these prayers for them.

Grandpa was the only person I ever knew who chose to regularly devote time to prayer by himself. I did hear other people praying at religious services, where they would read Hebrew in unison from their prayer books. I was pretty sure they didn't understand what they were saying any more than Grandpa did.

Children absorb a lot by osmosis. I absorbed the expression "Because we're Jewish" as a way of explaining to myself why we did what we did.

When I was growing up, the one thing I never, ever wondered about was God. I heard the word *God* mentioned in Sunday school, but Esther and Joseph were much more interesting because I could visualize them. My thick coloring books had pictures of Daniel in the lion's den, Noah building the ark, and Moses leading the people across the Red Sea. The Old Testament characters were fascinating. I heard the stories over and over until I knew them well. But none of this gave me the idea that God had anything to do with my real world. He seemed so impersonal—always too big, too high up, and too distant in every sense.

But my greatest delight in Sunday school was something other than the stories and lessons. To me, a box of sixty-four Crayola crayons (oh, the myriad of colors!) held the same delight as sixty-four thumbprint cookies with apricot centers.

As a little girl, I was *the* best colorist in my class. My skill at using crayons in that Bible coloring book led me to believe I had a rosy future. At least my teacher, Sonya Shapiro, implied that I did. "Pupils, look how perfectly Judy colors in the lines. Look at her Noah and the ark!" (Interestingly, Mrs. Shapiro was a bit prophetic regarding my future occupation.)

My impression of God was akin to the chandelier hanging in my friend Barbara's dining room. Though I had eaten at her table, I couldn't tell you anything about the light fixture. Barbara and I would be engrossed in conversation, ignoring and not caring about the light above our heads. Did we know there was a chandelier up there? Certainly. How else could we see each other or the lean corned beef on rye sandwiches with coleslaw and crisp kosher pickle?

So if you asked whether I thought there was a God, I'd have answered yes, just as I would have figured there was a chandelier over the table. I never stopped to appreciate the bright light (or God) and in fact never thought one thing about it (or God).

I honestly didn't care about this invisible person, but I definitely knew his name and used it daily—the same way everyone around me did—in vain. I heard people swear by his name and use it in many other situations that violated one of the Ten Commandments . . . which I did not know as a young person. "You are not to use lightly the name of ADONAI your God, because ADONAI will not leave unpunished someone who uses his name lightly" (CJB).

Not once did I feel shame for using God's name in this manner. Nor did I suspect that anyone else felt bad either. As a child in Sunday school, I had learned to write the word *God* as "G-d." I, the child-wonderer, didn't understand why God was too holy to have his name spelled out, but not holy enough for us to refrain from using his name freely when we were frustrated or angry.

In many ways, my life was the same as that of any young person, Jewish or Gentile. I loved to read, I loved going to movies, and—after the giant mahogany wonder arrived in our living room—I loved watching television.

The glamorous men and women I saw on the screen became my idols. The tiny candy store at the corner supplied me with penny candy and—most importantly—movie magazines. In my preteen years, the Crayolas fell by the wayside as my fingers became busy turning the pages of Hollywood monthlies. After reading every word, I would carefully cut out the full-page pictures of my favorite stars.

I accumulated hundreds of these photos and would spend hours admiring them and arranging them across my bedroom floor—sometimes even out onto the carpeting of the living and dining room. Each day I would reorganize the movie stars in different ways, according to gender, families, movie roles, etc., before carefully placing them back into boxes.

"Judy, pick those up so I can get to the kitchen!" (Daddy was yelling and again taking the Lord's name in vain.) Apparently the display was keeping Daddy from getting to his bagel, lox, and cream cheese sandwich—or maybe his kosher salami sandwich with potato salad on the side.

My fantasies became my whole world. I spent many hours pondering how to become a movie star or perhaps a classical ballerina. I persuaded my mother to let me take ballet lessons, but that proved a disaster, so I settled for tap dancing. Blue-eyed Ginger Rogers and slender Fred Astaire, dancing stars of dazzling musicals, were my mentors. (This was free of charge since they didn't know it.) I, too, was blue-eyed and slender, so I figured that would give me an edge in my career.

Although my black, patent-leather tap shoes hitting the linoleum kitchen floor brought out my star quality, it also brought out the worst in my daddy. He'd scream, "If you must tap, go tap your fingers on a table!"

I would yell back, "All right, I will. I'll do both. I'll tap on the floor and tap on the table at the same time! Thanks for the idea!"

Then I would tap out the front door and into the night air to avoid being killed.

This preteen lapse into Hollywood mania was my escape from the more complex parts of my life, including the strange fact that I had two moms and two dads and eight grandparents—not to mention one Russian great-grandpa.

No other Jewish family I knew had ever experienced divorce. I bore the weighty repercussions of a broken home. My last name differed from my mother's, since she had remarried, and I found this extremely embarrassing. My stepfather, whom I called "Daddy," was a rage-a-holic who frightened me; my aloof stepmother was cruel with words; and my father—a wealthy and brilliant court judge—was known as a cold, prideful man.

Gradually, however, even the wonderful fantasy world of Hollywood began to falter. My magazines printed stories that left me shocked and dismayed. My stars also had lives that were falling apart. Everything in me cried out, "Please live happily ever after—like in the movies!" I was sorely disillusioned.

Fortunately, a distraction was just around the corner . . .

CHAPTER 2

LIVING THE LIFE— THE JEWISH LIFE

My teenage years announced, "I'm here!" The braces came off, lipstick came on, and my string-bean shape picked up some curves. One thing that didn't change, though, was my penchant for wondering.

Yet I never had to spend time wondering why I wanted to attend shul (synagogue) every Friday evening. Those Shabbat (Sabbath) services brought me a religion I could finally believe in—boys. After thirteen-year-old boys had their Bar Mitzvah, many parents insisted they continue to attend shul on Friday nights. (The boys hadn't understood much of what they recited at their Bar Mitzvah. They knew about the holidays and whatever the rabbi taught of Judaism, but Bible familiarity was almost nil.)

My girlfriends and I longed to study our new creed, *sooo* we went where the boys were. I exchanged my tap shoes for

9

three-inch high heels, pulled my thick blondish waves into a trendy tight ponytail and showed up to worship at the altar of flirtation. My friends and I were ready to grow in our faith!

Since I was spiritually dead but artistic in nature, I spent my time in the pew studying the detailed woodwork and the beautiful trappings of the synagogue. When the Torah was brought out, I admired the gorgeous maroon velvet covering, embroidered in gold and silver.

Eventually, I'd retreat into boredom and fully anticipate the final song—*Adon Olam.* This was one of the most familiar hymns in the entire Jewish liturgy, but who understood what we were enthusiastically singing? I was happy to sing the hymn with gusto, because it signaled the benediction and the final big "Ah-mein" (Amen).

Immediately after this would come the Oneg Shabbat (the traditional term for "the pleasure of Shabbat") where I would grab some delicious finger pastries—maybe a prune Danish—and socialize. Chats with girlfriends or my latest "crush" covered a variety of topics and at times were deep and questioning, but the subject of conversing with or relating to God never came up.

Besides Friday nights, I would also attend services on the Jewish holidays. The rabbi's sermons sometimes covered the stories from the coloring books, albeit with an expanded vocabulary. More often, I learned about ancient customs and rabbinic admonitions. I was also encouraged to buy Israeli bonds and give money to plant trees in the Jewish homeland.

The rabbi obviously studied magazine and newspaper articles, since he made references to them often. He favored *Reader's Digest* stories the most. The majority of the congregation seemed to enjoy reading the very same magazine and connected well to the references the rabbi was making.

During the longer services, which were mostly in Hebrew, I was a particularly observant Jew—that is, to escape monotony, I'd start observing anything with artistic detail. Then, as I got older, I became more interested in watching the congregants around me. People appeared to be generally uninterested in the service. Women would be whispering together or writing out various reminder lists; men sometimes nodded off and snored.

Not surprisingly, I concluded that what went on in synagogue had little to do with real life. I once asked my father, who was both a judge and an observant Jew, "Why must I go to synagogue?"

"You're Jewish, that's why!"

"Why can't I shop on a Jewish holiday?"

"Because you're Jewish."

As usual, my father's response left me frustrated. To be honest, I was much more passionate about shopping than I was about Shabbat. I spent far more time thinking about how I could make money babysitting than about anything the rabbi had to say.

In each of the three movements of Judaism (reform, conservative, and orthodox), doing good works was the basis of our faith and the focus of religious activity. All three manifestations of the Jewish faith were in agreement that "help our people" was the mandate.

And I *was* a big help in my exclusively Jewish neighborhood—to the devout rabbi next door. He and his wife often hired me to babysit. That was "helping our people," along with remuneration for me!

By spending time in their home and comparing their lifestyle to my own, I ended up learning even more about what "being Jewish" meant. Though my grandparents and father were religious, my mother and stepfather weren't, even though they held to Jewish ways of expression and family life.

At the rabbi's, if a lamp was on when the sun set Friday evening, no one—not even I, the babysitter—was allowed to turn it off. The same was true about turning off the television or the stove. By the same token, when a lamp, television, or stove was off, I was not allowed to turn it on. The turning-off-and-on had to do with making changes to something chemically, i.e., starting a fire. Devout Jewish people did no such "work" on the Sabbath.

For the same reason, neither did they drive. In traditionally observant communities, a number of Shabbat restrictions affected how a person interacted with others. Travel by conveyance was banned, for example, and there were even limits on how far one could walk outside the city limits into unpopulated territory.

But there was one thing about the way Jewish people lived that always delighted me, and that was the wonderful food we ate. I well remember the delectable aromas wafting through my grandmother's home. A roast brisket was always the Friday night fare.

"Grandma, why are we having brisket again?"

"Honey, it's the roast of choice for Jewish people."

And the bread served with the brisket would be pumpernickel, Kaiser rolls sprinkled with poppy seeds, or seedless rye. I recall a time when, mouth full of brisket, I asked,

"Grandma, may I have some butter for my roll?"

She refused me.

"No butter tonight."

She explained that since we're kosher, we never mix dairy (milikh) with meat (fleshick). Having brisket meant butterless rolls. On the radio one day I heard a singer belt out these words, "When the roll is called up yonder . . . " which made me giggle and wonder what happens to the butter when the roll gets called up yonder.

Keeping kosher also meant using certain dishes and flatware for eating dairy and another set for eating meat. It even meant using certain towels to dry the dishes. Not enough cabinets to hold it all? No problem—we'd just tuck the surplus under the sofa or beds.

What was there about being Jewish that required us to do these strange things? For the most part, these practices made no sense to my practical mind. But at the same time, I did not bemoan the many blessings that came with our birthright.

For one thing, we were a very tight-knit community. Besides eating together—a lot—we took care of each other. We conversed endlessly, thinking nothing of interrupting or finishing each other's sentences. We also loved to celebrate—holidays, weddings, Bar Mitzvahs, and any other reason we could think of to have a good time.

We lived Jewish, dated Jewish, married Jewish, educated our children Jewish, and lived in Jewish communities. There was a depth of connection stirring inside of us all. Warm, gregarious, humorous, expressive, hugging, and kissing—that's what life was. I loved my culture, loved the sentiments, the courage, and the survival. If you were around me long enough, you'd recognize from whence I came. I oozed it!

Jewish life was also kvetching (complaining), kvelling (delightedly gushing)—and worrying. A Jewish telegram might read: "Begin worrying. Details to follow."

Another important Jewish mainstay was what I like to call "Jewish acupuncture"—needling one's children. Here's a story to illustrate.

A man calls his mother in Florida.

"Mom, how are you?"

"Not too good," says the mother. "I've been very weak."

"Why are you so weak?"

She says, "Because I haven't eaten in thirty-eight days."

The man says, "That's terrible. Why haven't you eaten in thirty-eight days?"

The mother answers, "Because I didn't want my mouth to be filled with food if you should call."

No question, the very best part of my heritage was the laughter.

What became clear to me as I grew older was that there were two kinds of people in the world. There were Jews, and then there was everybody else. The "others" were the Gentiles. We weren't exactly hostile toward them, but we understood they were very different from us. They had their god, Jesus, and we had ours (the real God). They had their Bible, their holidays, their way of life. And we had ours.

As a child, I personally encountered Christianity only a few times. My parents would drive our big navy Buick Special through the Gentile neighborhoods during Christmas so I could gaze in wonder at the shining lights and decorations. One time I remember seeing a baby doll in a manger on someone's lawn.

"Mother, who's that baby in the crib?"

"That's Jesus."

So to me, Jesus was just a baby—a Gentile baby on Gentile lawns at Christmas.

Then at nineteen, while on a movie date, I got my first glimpse of a church interior. There on the screen was an emaciated gray cement figure hanging on a cross. I thought about that a long time. I wondered why anyone would want to worship a god who was dead.

CHAPTER 3

THE WHERE AND WHY YEARS

I never once thought, *What will happen to me when I die?*

Though I was curious by nature . . . I didn't ever ponder that subject, much less bother to ask anyone for an answer. The hereafter wasn't even a blip on the radar for me or anyone I knew—with all the files in my brain, there was none labeled "Eternity." But there was one titled, "Eat, Drink and Be Merry for Tomorrow We Die." With that as my guiding philosophy, I lived for the present, as if there were no Tomorrowland.

The only time I was exposed to the reality of time without end was at Jewish funerals, when it was natural for the subject to be brought up. The attending clergy might mention *heaven* or *hereafter* in his sermon. For me, those words had a superficiality, a perfunctory feel to them. "He's in a far better place," the rabbi would assure the somber group of family and friends. No details, however, were ever shared about that "place."

Why would that scholarly man use those words? How would he know where dead people went? It would appear the former life and behavior of the departed one was of no consequence—he may have wreaked havoc in his family or in his business dealings. Even so, at his funeral I'd hear, ". . . gone to a far better place." My inner response was, *Ho-hum. Let's get this over with, Rabbi.* I couldn't see myself ever being excited about a place that required me to die in order to go there. Rather than seriously considering the futuristic stuff, I wanted to eat, drink, and be merry. Some may have been having thoughts like, *What am I living for?* or *Is there something beyond this world?* I wasn't.

Heaven and *hell* were terms used in jest or as clichés among my friends, on television, and in films. Therefore, those two abodes seemed irrelevant to me. And if by chance there happened to be any actual eternal destination places, it seemed obvious enough that Hitler would be in hell, and I—along with all good people like me—would be in heaven.

Where had I gotten the idea that I was good, that I had a good soul? I well recall the particular service when our rabbi, in his rich, deep voice, informed our class of pre-teens, "You're all basically good. You weren't born with a sinful nature since you're created in the image of God. Oh yes, we all make mistakes, but this isn't our natural inclination. The world is simply messed up because people make wrong choices."

His powerful declaration became rooted deep in my psyche. Whatever the rabbi taught, I believed to be "gospel truth" and vital to the Judaic faith.

But contending against the rabbi's man-is-good tenet was this haunting "heart reality check," whispering, *If I do indeed have a good heart, then what about this inclination to wrong thinking, speaking, and behavior? From where inside of me does that originate? If my nature is a good one, then why do I have this natural inclination to sin? If I'm good, why do I have thoughts, speak words, and do things that I don't feel right about?*

This paradox haunted me for years. The rabbi's declaration confused my young heart. Yet, because it was all I knew, I lived with this code. As time passed, I sensed that people viewed their sins as little more than mistakes, misfortunes, or some kind of maladjustment.

When my mother remarried, I became subject to a significant code variation. Reform Judaism, with its religious liberality, became the new practice in our home, replacing a more traditional version.

In spite of my family's involvement with diverse views, I was still clear about my spiritual identity. Judaism was 4,000 years old and one of the major faiths in the world. For us modern Jews, performance was the deeply entrenched focus of acceptable religious expression. And of the good works we engaged in, philanthropy in particular was considered one of the ultimate forms. The reminders were constant and consistent—to be charitable to one another, ever helping those less fortunate than ourselves, and to perpetually support Israel.

Having grown up hearing Jews identified as the "Chosen People," I assumed that God loved the Jewish populace and the homeland he designated for them. But I never had any understanding of him loving *me*—Judy—personally. Even if I thought such a connection was possible, I'd have wondered how he could ever love *me*—Judy—since my core was so flawed.

I didn't know if my friends were "wondering Jews" like me, since none ever spoke of spiritual matters. As an ethnic clan, we were "good works" oriented, but all were totally silent when it came to faith. God and belief were subjects never broached among my peers.

By the time I was twenty, I had learned about the different divisions of my religion and the widely varied philosophies of each. But despite vast discrepancies in practice, there was one important area of agreement uniting *all* branches—Jewish food!

No matter whether you are orthodox, conservative, or reform, the consensus is that Jewish dishes are extraordinary. Mouth-watering apple cake, chopped liver, gefilte fish, pickled herring, tzimmes (a Jewish vegetable stew), challah (braided egg bread), knishes, stuffed cabbage, bagels and lox, blintzes, latkes (potato pancakes), matzo ball soup, beef brisket and kugel (noodle pudding) connect us all. The dishes are lovingly fried, baked, broiled, steamed, or simmered—skillfully prepared by Jewish mothers, of course. The chant "Eat! Eat!" echoes with gusto in most Yiddish homes.

But once a year, the chant changes to "Fast! Fast!" These deny-yourself words signal the arrival of Yom Kippur, a most holy day of fasting, confession and repentance. Because of its cultural significance, many secular Jews observe this holiday even if they opt out of most others. On the Day of Atonement, synagogue attendance soars!

Traditionally, observance begins at dusk the night before and ends as the sun sets the following day. There is no eating or drinking, no bathing or brushing teeth, no anointing oneself with perfumes or lotions, and no marital relations. The nation of Israel actually shuts down all radio and television broadcasts, all public transportation, and all airports.

By the time my teenage years arrived, I was joining with millions of Jewish people in the Yom Kippur fast. Sadly for me, the abstention from food stimulated no spiritual thoughts. Rather, my mind was fixated on the "no eating, drinking, bathing, or teeth brushing." I longed for the sun to go down so I might break the fast with a feast served up by the family matriarchs. With no cooking skills, I just contributed toothpicks. The cooks were amused for sure.

During the services, while frequently checking my watch, I'd question silently, *How much longer must I suffer through this day?* Pride, sitting right alongside me, offered some spiritually pacifying commentary: "You're such a good Jew. You're fasting twenty-four hours and spending most of the day in synagogue. Good for you, Judy!" I heartily agreed.

Those hours in synagogue included standing painfully still in my high heels, with Siddur (prayer book) in hand, for what seemed like an eternity. I joined in with the rest of the congregation, reading aloud the abundant list of sins from my thin-paged volume. It was customary to gently beat one's chest while confessing sins. This was as if to say your heart may have led you astray in the past, but hopefully it will not happen again.

I realize the Jewish scholars who wrote these words of supplication never meant for them to be vain repetitions. They wrote poetic words, precise and poignant, for Jewish people like me to pour out in sincere contrition on this holy day. Repentance was not to be just a fleeting thought like other impressions that come and go in a person's mind.

Every so often I did take ownership of a sin, but it was with a shallowness of soul. The exercise of repentance was obligatory for all, but at best, it was just cursory for me. I merely spoke the words as hollow reiterations.

I was young and unable to resonate with or even comprehend many transgressions on the list, so the holiday was anything but worrisome for me. Other than maybe a few fleeting moments of remorse, I had no reason to take it seriously. Besides, why be concerned about so-called forgiveness from a God I never knew or thought about?

Added to all this irrelevance, the drone of public confession made me sleepy on my feet. It took more than ten minutes to read through the sin liturgy. Some congregants would be reading aloud, all at their own pace, so the sanctuary reverberated with indistinguishable muttering, occasionally punctuated by a recognizable word or two. I would quicken my reading at times or slow it down, making an effort to stay on course with the hundreds in the pews. Obviously, my heart was more engaged with reading aloud correctly than with confession and repentance.

The reason to pray together, reciting each sin, was so that the congregation as a whole might attain true atonement. Being totally self-centered, however, I wasn't reading with that perspective at all. Instead, logic made me ask, *Why must I read all these sins when the majority of them have nothing to do with me?* With that rationale, on this holy day, I deduced that my personal good outweighed the bad.

Each Yom Kippur, I'd think about who would make the cut on God's measuring stick, and who wouldn't. I reasoned, *Hitler is who you would call bad; I am good since my sins are, first of all, so few. What's more, they don't fall in the category of murder, bank-robbery or prostitution. Of course, I do lie and reveal secrets at times, but what's wrong with a little white lie or gossip among friends, anyway?*

As with my view of heaven, I use the words *superficial* and *perfunctory* to describe how I thought about forgiveness from this invisible and unknowable God—a distant God who was no part of my life or reality. Since I had no vibrant, personal, living relationship with him, I was focused on myself alone, bored with the religiosity of the whole day. The tedious morning-to-evening Hebrew services, my empty stomach, and my dry, mint-less mouth left me totally uninterested in this holiday.

I subsequently reasoned that since Yom Kippur was observed only once in 365 days, I would simply be a nominal participant—though maybe I would at least try to read more in unison with everyone next year.

To complete the picture, I'll add one practical observation: Sadly, by the time a number of congregants left synagogue to break the "fast," normal familial criticizing, prickly conversations, and *kvetching* (complaining), were back in full force. People had—just minutes before—hugged and kissed at the close of the service; they'd entreated God to mercifully absolve them of their wrongdoing. And now, almost instantly, the tentacles of sin were enslaving them again!

CHAPTER 4

JUDY-OF-ALL-TRADES

If my rabbi's words weren't enough to convince me I had an intrinsic good character, there was always plenty of validation from others that should have been able to do the trick. Exclamations like these were plentiful:

"We love Judy!"

"What a delightful young lady!"

"What a great student to have in my classroom!"

"What a lovely daughter you're raising!"

At times my mother took a different view: "What a whiner you are! What a sassy mouth you have!" But away from the house, no one saw that side of me. I always *un-whined* as soon as my feet hit the pavement outside. I also made sure to shut off the sass.

From the time I sat in kindergarten with politely folded hands, through subsequent years of raising my hand to spout correct answers, my teachers called me a "brain."

Becoming the first female editor-in-chief of the high school newspaper afforded me much acclaim, as did being the recipient of the prestigious Daughters of the American Revolution Award. A Jewish student like me didn't appear to be a likely candidate for the award, since my forefathers fought the Philistines . . . not the Brits (!).

In the business arena, I was voted president of Junior Achievement, where we teenagers founded a company and learned how to run it from the bottom up. Our business produced dozens upon dozens of wooden plant holders. Because of that endeavor, I have never wanted a plant of any kind in my home!

On the sports scene, as the lone Jewish teammate, I played right wing for varsity hockey and center forward for varsity basketball. Hitting hockey pucks and slam-dunking on the court kept me extremely busy after school. The applause meter kept going up, up, up. *I'm a pretty good kid*, I would try to convince myself.

Even at summer camp, everything I touched turned to gold. From the age of five through sixteen, I was sent away for eight weeks to Pennsylvania's Pocono Mountains. I captained the volleyball team, hit bulls-eyes with bow and arrow, shot targets dead-center with a rifle, won ribbons in horse shows, and was chosen leader of a major activity (Color War) that we campers considered the high point of the summer. Being selected for this honor was a dream come true. The luck of the Irish! I mean to say, the luck of the Jewish!

So performance triumphs were many, but personality also factored into my success story. From the time I starting pulling childhood pranks, classmates always seemed to want me around. Who wouldn't be drawn to the laughter and comedic pauses that brighten a dull school day?

"Funny" was in the genes. I was genetically equipped for comedy, thanks to my mother, who was the queen of high jinks. How well I remember looking forward to introducing my mother to a new date. As I ushered him into the living room, there was my strikingly beautiful and stylishly dressed mom seated primly on our sofa, reading the Philadelphia Inquirer—which she was holding upside down.

Other times, she might stuff her mouth with a banana right before I'd introduce her to a new boy, and out would squirt the squishy yellow stuff along with "Nice to meet you, Gordon."

I was often compared to the popular comedienne of the day, Carol Burnett. By high school's end, I was voted "The Most Popular Girl in the Senior Class." The title was like chocolate icing on a yellow cake (my favorite dessert).

Celebrated as I was academically, athletically, and socially, I would feast on the praise and nourish my hungry heart with it, tacking the compliments to the wall of my heart. There was a perplexing problem though: The accolades wouldn't stick to my ribcage, wherein lay my heart.

At 10:30 p.m., when day was done and no one was around, I would find myself confronted with the true Judy. Hockey uniform dropped to the floor, latest award dropped on the dresser, and me dropped in bed—that is where I met myself, *my real self.* Any vanity began to dissipate. The room was pitch dark, and so was my mood.

What became clear in the silence was a disease festering in the inner recesses of my moral fiber. Sometime the symptom was jealousy. Maybe another night I'd come face to face with my resentments, or possibly greed. At times I clearly saw my selfishness, lust, or covetousness.

As I lay on my bed each night, the reality of my true inner nature could not be pushed aside by brilliant reasoning or sparkling humor. I surmised that the true spirit of a person is best known in the dark. I wondered if there were others lying in the dark who, like me, were aware of the inner workings of their heart.

For many years I asked myself, *If I have a good heart, then where is the wrong thinking, speaking, and behaving coming from?* Though I was deemed smart, popular, successful, a good Jew, and well loved, I knew in my "knower" there was darkness lurking within—a darkness that overshadowed all the acclamations.

Even as a young girl, I innately knew validation was foundational for me. Without my bright reputation, I would certainly collapse into someone looking flatter than a yeastless matzo cracker. Even my outstanding credentials bolstered by the rabbi's words were unable to topple my strong conviction of a flawed heart within. All the honors, all the complimentary words rang untrue by bedtime.

Alone at night, there was no feeling of worth, significance, or adequacy. My façade, which others found so dazzling, just couldn't squelch the condemnation that was coming from somewhere. *From where, though? How do I fix it? Or should I just stifle or ignore what I'm seeing?*

I wasn't depressed. Lack of confidence wasn't the problem. I had every reason to feel secure. Look at my life résumé! Then why, when alone, separated from the acclaim, did I feel this lament, this wretchedness of soul, this emptiness inside?

The basic longing for self-worth is to be accepted, loved, needed, missed, understood, cared for, and appreciated. That's what causes a person to feel important and special. Yes, the world was giving me a semblance of self-worth. But then why wasn't I happy when I put my thick hair (yes, I even had great hair) on the pillow at night?

The Jewish *wonderer* thought maybe there was some kind of wisdom, some hidden truth to salve this disquiet. *Go to the rabbi, Judy.* No, no. The rabbi had already spoken to this subject. But inwardly, I didn't measure up to his words—in those dark hours, night after night, "The Most Popular Girl" felt unclean.

Like most of my friends' parents, mine valued education above all else. My father cited our family's background as a way to motivate me. "Your grandparents left the homeland with nothing but the clothes on their backs. You must study and work hard to succeed."

So I became a super-studier and super-achiever. In the Jewish community of my day, a college degree was seen as the ticket to power and prosperity. Financial security equaled protection and status, so the ability to make money was held in enormously high regard. Of course, if you didn't make money, you could always marry it. My mother hoped for a son-in-law who was a doctor or dentist. "It's just as easy to marry a rich man as a poor one," she'd tell me. "A Dr. Goldberg or a Dr. Schwartz would be nice, dear. I only want the best for you, *Joodala*."

At graduation I was chosen to honor our principal on behalf of the senior class. I gave a few well-rehearsed comments and sat down. As one of my classmates stood to sing, "You'll Never Walk Alone," I fought hard to restrain the tears. The words and melody were rich and stirred memories of exceptional school days, but never did my thoughts go to God in gratefulness. Though it was an emotional few minutes for me, my spirit remained numb.

And for my proud father, the icing on his cake was discovering that he'd be spared a huge expenditure. Because my grades were in the top percentile, my name was announced as the recipient of a four-year academic scholarship to the college of my choice—a surprise to me, too!

CHAPTER 5

HITTING THE CAMPUS

As high school ended, I felt unclean and somehow heart-stained. Remembering how my mother used to take a bar of soap to clean out my "sass mouth," I wondered if there was a similar remedy for my heart.

But for the moment, I put that uneasiness on hold, as I had something new to occupy my thoughts: college. I decided to use my scholarship at the University of Maryland, a school near Washington, D.C. The stately Georgian architecture and verdant campus were eye candy to me.

The diversion of college and all it had to offer temporarily pushed back concerns about my authentic self—about not being the person I wanted to be.

There wasn't time to try and settle that issue, since I literally had a *major* dilemma—what to choose as my college major. My mother and I laughingly ruled out looking for majors related to the recent past—like plant container development from my Junior Achievement days.

"Don't mention the word "plant" to me, Mom!"

She chuckled and replied, "Judy, how about hockey stick design?"

"Yeh, how about pink jeweled-studded sticks?"

We bantered back and forth for awhile. A sensible consideration would have been journalism because of my post as editor-in-chief of the school paper.

That reasoning took a sharp, unexpected turn when, days later, I heard these words: "You've got it, Judy!" My friend's mother, a successful painter, looked through my school art portfolio and made up my mind for me. Hearing, "You've got promising talent!" was all the motivation I needed to major in art at the huge Maryland university.

To learn my trade, I used paints, pastels, pens, papier-mâché, plastics, polymers, Play-Doh, plaster, and plywood. I studied palaces and painters from Picasso to Pissarro. For four fantastic years everything I wore was perpetually tinged with clay, chalk, glue, ink, watercolors, and oils. My clothing now bore the same attribute as my heart—stained.

I regularly spent July and August off as a certified Red Cross swimming and boating instructor in the Poconos—my summer stomping grounds for most of my life. I enthusiastically taught untold numbers of youth to float, blow bubbles underwater, swim every stroke in the book, surface dive to the bottom of the lake, and—most importantly—how to save a life. My job had me outside, baking in the heat all day long. With what we now know about sun damage, it's a miracle that my skin never turned to leather. (I could have been a great jacket, not exactly Italian quality leather, but perhaps a nice faux).

Planning swim meets was grueling. Loudly cheering the teams had me popping lozenges daily. I commonly returned home in August with the reward of laryngitis. My witty mom would comment, "At least you won't talk back for a while." No wonder she kept encouraging me to work far away at camp!

Yes, I was an expert swimmer, but spiritually, I never took the plunge. There was no interest, as things were going swimmingly in my life without assistance.

The outside world was ever affirming that I was *naturally* a good person and did everything well. I recall the day at camp when an elderly man watched me take an arrow from my quiver and shoot it with precision. He yelled out, "That girl is some good!" Isn't that exactly what the rabbi asserted about my spirit? In fact, I could see a correlation between sharpshooting and life itself: It seemed evident that no matter where I aimed my arrows, they landed right on target. Because I knew that nobody likes a bad person—thank goodness I was highly esteemed and in no danger of being labeled as "bad." In fact, the only one who felt otherwise about Judy was Judy!

Once each Pennsylvania summer drew to a close, I would return to college, which of course involved lots of new experiences. As a freshman, I had naturally begun to encounter and learn about the Gentile world that had previously been pretty foreign to me. I really came to enjoy my classmate Jim Henson, creator of the Muppets as well as a significant part of the international TV hit *Sesame Street*. We "puppeted" together, fashioning marionettes and putting on shows in class. Henson's Kermit the Frog truly turned Jim into a prince of a man. And his future Miss Piggy was the first pork this Jewish girl ever liked!

In that same puppetry class, a platonic relationship began between me and another talented non-Jewish guy. John took me to his fraternity dances, where I came face-to-face (and feet-to-feet) with plenty of Gentiles. Using mallets and metal nutcrackers, my date and I worked on renowned Maryland steamed crabs while working on getting to know each other. I was now enjoying non-kosher seafood *and* enjoying a non-kosher boy!

My parents had no clue. Why ruin their days? Although I knew I must marry a Jewish man, it was thrilling to break out from the unwritten but common boundaries. The Jewish tenet to keep the "goyim" at a distance was so ingrained that I was half scared when tempted with this forbidden fruit named John.

Now my wondering had a new focus. *Would John attack me? Was there something really immoral about him? What's so wrong with Gentile boys?*

Often I would interrogate John about Christianity. To my surprise, he didn't understand his religion any better than I did mine. We compared our various traditions and laws, but neither of us had any real sense of who God was, what he could do, or what was written in the Bible.

Then one sunny autumn day, as I approached my huge, columned AEΦ sorority house, I spotted him on the porch. No, not Gentile John, but gentle Jewish Bernie. He and his virile, v-neck-sweatered roommate were playing bridge with my cute, cashmere-sweatered sorority sisters. One look at Bernie and infatuation zapped me. From then on, this "secret love" was ever in the background. Bernie from Baltimore had strangely invaded my thoughts.

He was a star athlete, a three-letter man with the coveted title "All Maryland State Quarterback." Bernie had also tried out for the New York Yankees, which made him ever so "cool," not to mention popular. He'd even been voted "Best Looking" in high school. I certainly would have given him my vote.

Can you believe that for a whole year, Bernie ignored me? But eventually, the silence was broken. On the last day of finals, outside the mammoth math building, the charmer made a remark about my bright yellow-and-white outfit. Then followed . . .

"What are you doing this summer?"

"I'm the swim instructor for a camp in the Poconos."

"If you give me your address, I'll drop you a line."

Sweetest words this side of heaven—not that I even thought there *was* a heaven. Bernie and I corresponded throughout the summer, rapidly fanning the spark of attraction into a full-blown blaze.

At graduation, I acquired a B.A in art education and not long after, an M-R-S. Like many Jewish young men, Bernie went on to law school; I went on to teach art. Despite her earlier aspirations for a son-in-law, my mother wasn't terribly disappointed when I ended up with Bernie the attorney, as a lawyer was her third choice, after neurosurgeon or orthodontist.

As we embarked on married life, I made some unanticipated discoveries about Bernie. They all boiled down to him being actually *more* wonderful than I'd even realized. This new husband was easy-going, unselfish, never demanding, never complaining, and never critical. As a result, I felt miserable! Not because of who Bernie was, but because of who I wasn't.

Compared to my difficult father, step-mother and step-father, I didn't appear to be *that* bad. But placed alongside easy-going Bernie—well, that was a different story. He was the nicest person I had ever known. I wanted to be more like this man.

Bernie, unknowingly, had moved me to find a remedy for my heart condition. A bypass wouldn't do. I, the born wonderer, began to wonder at full throttle. I had a goal, but where to go for help? How to effect a cure?

CHAPTER 6

CAN'T SAY I DIDN'T TRY

Finances are the great fix-all. Who hasn't been exposed to this logic? Who hasn't considered this worldview? *Fiddler*'s Tevya warbled, "If I were a rich man . . . " That was obviously *his* mindset.

The day our twins Jeff and Jill were born, Bernie the attorney opened his own law practice, which meant money in the bank. After years of law school and working for someone else, this would be a welcome change. But, it was actually more than change; it was dollars—lots of them. The idea of plentiful cash helped me formulate a plan. Money could be the key to validation, to raising one's status. And lots of money, I figured, could surely bring feelings of significance. I wondered if getting new "things"—the very latest, the very best—would bring increased contentment in life. Why not try? Why not soak money for all it is worth?

I soaked it with a sizable addition to our house, private schooling for the children, signature clothing in my closet, a Lincoln Town Car in the driveway, and a glorious ocean condo in Florida. Admiration did increase.

"Thanks for letting us stay in your condo. You are so lucky to have it!"

"Oh, I love the way your drapes blend perfectly with the apricot carpeting. Where did you find that fabric?"

"I love your children's outfits. Where do you shop?"

"Your car drives like a dream. I love the navy interior and that new car smell."

As a twosome, my husband and I were sought after socially, and our calendar was always full. One particular night remains etched in my memory. Bernie and I had arrived home after a lavish country club event. A stunning tulle and black lace flouncy cocktail dress had been the perfect choice for the dinner dance. I stood before my mirror, still in the elegant dress, and began to remove a sparkling earring by the light of a small lamp.

Suddenly, my fingers stopped fiddling, and as I stood there motionless, these thoughts flooded in: *The evening feels like such a waste. Our weekends are full of parties and dining out, but I come home feeling so empty. Is this all there is? Nothing else? Is there no greater purpose?*

My life feels so darn shallow. I adore my friends, but our hectic social life rings hollow. So what is wrong with me? I'm tired of going from gathering to gathering, from eatery to eatery, with almost identical chit-chat. It's always centered on raising children, golf and tennis games, the latest news around town, sports scores, movies, television shows, and the best vacation spots. The small talk, the teasing and jokes have sameness. I'm tired of hearing, "Judy, you're such a riot." There must be something more!

I was sobered by these strong feelings. My, oh my, where did they come from? I finished removing my earrings, placed my diamond rings and watch in the gold-leaf jewelry box, hung my designer dress on a scented, padded hanger, and returned my expensive black silk high heels to their see-through shoe box. I had now removed all the outer splendor of who I was.

Once in bed that night, I wondered why, now that I was a wealthy woman, the praises birthed from added luxuries wouldn't fasten to my soul. The intoxicating compliments seemed to unstick as quickly as they came. Like a puff of smoke.

A few weeks earlier, while immersed in a novel, I read a line that grabbed my attention, and I jotted it on the pad next to my phone. Now that sentence came back to me: "What benefit will it be to you if you gain the whole world but lose your own soul?" I desired "soul gain" and though the additional material things brought great conveniences, I gained nothing in the heart area. Adding more trimmings to my life, which money facilitated, would never be enough to award me a new heart, a pure spirit. I was again left alone with those ever-present feelings of insignificance and emptiness. More status with people, yes. But with myself, no. I was finding that even as Bernie's salary kept increasing, money didn't satisfy.

So my next stop on the road towards self-fulfillment was to busy myself with new skills and fresh activities. I learned to scuba dive, but gave it up because of a concern for the bends—a diver's disease with horrific consequences. Afraid this malady might be waiting for me under the sea, I said my goodbyes to the heavy oxygen tank.

Next, I joined an acting group called "The Spotlighters," only to give it up after the first play. The rehearsals were terribly time-consuming. In addition, inviting people who'd paid good money to hear me say, "Would you like your tea on the veranda or in the gazebo?" was embarrassing. Having been cast in the lowly role of a parlor maid, I figured a starched white apron could be worn at home just as well. So I took leave of Broadway.

Then I took a crack at knitting. To my delight, I was able to produce several sweaters—albeit poorly fitting ones. The worst was when I knit three cashmere wool sleeves for my two-armed husband! Because of the costly mistake, there wasn't enough yarn left to cover Bernie's back. My attempt at knitting now came to an abrupt, expensive end. I said my goodbyes to the knitting needles.

What came next was snow skiing. I gave it a try and gave it up. A fall on the mountain left ligaments torn and tendons pulled. I didn't even know I had ligaments and tendons. While in the hospital, in horrific pain, I swore off the slopes and bid adieu to my ski poles.

Sewing would be safer. Why not give it a try? After learning the "Stretch and Sew" method, I made many matching outfits for Jill and Jeff, pajamas for Mark and Johnny, and T-shirts for Bernie. The twins wore their outfits; their siblings rejected the pajamas (preferring to sleep in underwear), and Bernie ignored his cotton-knit Ts since the sleeves dug into his armpits. After several months, I gave up the colored spools because it wasn't worth the time it took to keep ripping and starting over! Au revoir, Singer sewing machine.

My last attempt at proving my "Skills Add Worth" maxim was to master the tap dancing of my childhood. The lessons were great fun and my progress was impressive. Problem was, my black patent tap shoes scratched the floor and added to the din of an already noisy environment populated by four outgoing children. So did I say any goodbyes to "brush, step, shuffle, ball change"? No, because I still like to tap (though in private, for sure).

How I picked up all of these skills in about two years' time was surprising. I was taken aback at something else, too. At 10:30 p.m., when the tap shoes were off and I lay in bed, it was apparent that even with tap dancing and all that wealth, I was still left feeling unworthy. My inherent flaws were untouched by knitting, scuba diving, skiing, sewing, acting, dancing, and the rest.

Then at some point, a new thought emerged as a remedy for my heart condition. Money obviously wasn't the answer, nor was adding different abilities to my "portfolio"; the problem must be *selfishness*! I needed to be doing things for other people. Why hadn't I seen this blazing truth before? I reproved myself, *Move away from self-centered living, Judy!*

So I joined the National Council of Jewish Women and plunged into charity work. Through fund-raising efforts, we met a lot of needs within the Jewish community here and in Israel. Visiting orphanages with gifts kept me busy. Wherever there was a job to be done, I was ready to volunteer. Because the leaders were pleased with my diligence, they appointed me to the Maryland board of the nationwide organization.

When I was notified about the position, I was thrilled. It was not so much the honor that excited me, but rather that now I might be able to learn what made these "cream of the crop" women tick. I wanted to know what made them so *good*.

At the same time, I had to admit to feeling a bit guilty about my prestigious appointment. If they had known what I was really like, they'd never have me on the board. I devised a strategy whereby these outstanding women would mentor me—without them even knowing it. I assumed this elite group had it all together, and they probably assumed the same of me. From the very first gathering, I closely observed the way they operated and how they handled people and situations. I also listened closely to their speech.

Then ever so gradually, it began to dawn on me that we were no different! Most of them were prideful and filled with anxiety. I also witnessed a lot of petty behavior, including the common lunchtime activity of gossiping. When all was said and done, I didn't want their mentoring. I gave up the post after serving one year, but continued in the organization for a while.

Setting aside the certificates honoring me for volunteer work, I'd slide under the covers at my normal 10:30 p.m. Once there, though cozy and comfy externally, my heart still checked out the same—unchanged.

A glance back over the past few years really baffled me. With all my valiant and consistent efforts, I wasn't transformed. My old flaws weren't gone; if anything, they were expanding. And new ones were pushing through.

Were any of my much-loved friends questioning what made *them* tick? I wondered if all of us who had so much going outwardly were too proud or embarrassed to reveal our inner motivations. On the other hand, maybe no one else was in touch with the still waters that ran deep. In my case, there was no depression, no neurosis, no psychoanalyzing (I wouldn't have known how). It was just that my failings were popping up all over the place for me to see.

My life was beginning to feel like Whack-a-Mole—the arcade game where a plastic mole pops up from one of five holes at random. The object is to force the creature back down by hitting it on the head. But then, of course, the mole simply pops up somewhere else. I was an accident on the way to happen with what popped up next . . .

CHAPTER 7

OUT OF THIS WORLD

My mother was on the phone with an animated announcement: "I've just finished an absolutely life-changing book. You must get it!" Absolutely change my life? A cautious hope began to stir in my heart.

My thoughts were whirling as she enthusiastically described Maxwell Maltz's book *Psychocybernetics*. Mom was sold on the author's theories about the mind's inner powers being stronger than normal thinking.

Nothing in my life had ever lured me to investigate anything beyond the visible and practical. My search for answers had been limited to the tangible, material world in which I'd been raised. I saw only the natural part of the universe, and interpreted truth against that background.

As a twelve-year-old, though, I did once pick up a book about hypnotism, which I found in our home. Very little of it made sense to me; still, I remember being fascinated by the idea that there might be something more than what we experience in our ordinary lives.

As soon as I hung up the phone, I scurried to the bookstore and returned with the hardback. Once settled in my black leather recliner with some chocolates and the book (great combination), I was transported to a heretofore unknown "other" world. My worldview was about to change.

The author insisted I could become, for example, a great basketball player if I daily sat visualizing myself shooting and scoring baskets. Yes! This was the sort of instruction, the how-to magic, I had been looking for all these years—I'd wanted someone to tell me that I, Judy, had the power to change myself.

"*Psychocybernetics* led me to even deeper wells: it touched on Dale Carnegie's theories about positive thinking. So I rushed out to buy those books, which launched me into practicing new mental techniques.

At this time there was a heightened public interest in the supernatural, so it wasn't long before I began to read fascinating newspaper and magazine accounts about ESP (Extra Sensory Perception) and mental telepathy. It made sense that the reason people were dissatisfied with this life was because they were designed to go beyond the ordinary into mystical, paranormal realms.

Yoga classes were forming in Baltimore, so I went to the local YWCA to join in. Daily I did the physical postures and breathing exercises, which included meditating and chanting a special mantra. My yoga books promised that if I was faithful in the physical and spiritual disciplines, all maladies of any sort would dissolve. A brand-new Judy would emerge.

Yoga became central, and the other women in the class became my close friends. We were reading the same books and asking the same questions. For many months I tried to be diligent about meditating. I would shut myself in my room and endeavor to reach a spiritual enlightenment the gurus called *Nirvana*. But first I had to empty my mind of distractions like, *What should I serve for dinner?* or *Did I turn the dishwasher on?* In most instances, rather than connecting with a supreme force, I was rewarded with the desire to take a nap or eat a chocolate chip cookie.

Now that a momentum had begun, it was only a matter of time before I added astrology to my life. I visited an astrologer in Washington, D.C. and paid her a good amount of money to do a chart, not only on myself but also on the rest of my family. Days later, I located a nearby personal prognosticator whom I thereafter visited regularly to obtain predictions about my future.

I was not delving into the supernatural world as a thrill seeker, but was truly seeking a blameless heart. I gave myself fully to this world because all my forays into the material, visible, tangible world produced no success. Why *not* try the paranormal and invisible realms?

My motivating desire was to get into bed at night feeling squeaky clean, as if I had just stepped out of a "heart" shower. I longed to be free and unburdened. But no one else seemed to understand my dilemma. Whenever I tried to explain that my failings were the reason for my search, friends would respond:

"Judy, that's nothing!"

"I'm the same way! What's the big deal?"

"You're a terrific person. What are you talking about?"

Though baited by their reasoning, my mind refused to yield. With renewed vigor, I redirected my questioning pursuits from self-serving materialism to soul-searching mysticism. To find spiritual reality apart from my intellect and natural senses was my goal. "Deeper" and "higher" were the buzz words. If this could transform my core, I was poised to buy into it—hook, line and sinker.

Getting swallowed up by unorthodox religious offshoots took a giant leap forward on my next visit to the library. (The many-windowed tan brick building had been a happy hangout from the time I could first ride a bike.) There, my attention was drawn to the biography of Edgar Cayce, a 20th century trance medium. I pulled a hard wooden chair up to a deeply grained oak table, sat down, and eagerly scanned the pages. Minutes later I checked the book out with a greater thirst for hidden knowledge than when I first entered the cavernous building.

That evening, once the four children were bathed and bedded, I devoured the book. I learned that as a young man, Cayce developed severe laryngitis. No remedies proved curative, so he turned to a hypnotist. From his earliest sessions, rather than simple hypnotism, Cayce was experiencing some sort of supernatural "possession." While he was in an altered state, his voice would return. This allowed him to speak on behalf of spirits who would diagnose ailments and prescribe successful treatments for Cayce's followers, often when his only contact with the afflicted person was by mail. Word got out, which precipitated an influx of people writing letters or traveling (even from overseas) to receive guidance and remedies from the "sleeping prophet."

The more I studied Cayce's books, the more I became convinced he had discovered the truth I was seeking. It wasn't long before I opened my home on a weekly basis to those who wanted to explore, discuss, and experiment with Cayce's "readings." Eagerly absorbing his teachings, our group tightly bonded as months turned into years. All such gatherings were named "Search for God" groups by Cayce's foundation, but in all honesty, a God search wasn't my target. I was still just looking for whatever magic would free me from my sinful nature.

During thousands of trances, Cayce also spoke of things unrelated to health problems. He began to interpret dreams and make prophetic statements concerning the future. Perhaps most significantly, Cayce was known for expounding the theory of reincarnation. Interestingly, he initially resisted this idea but eventually decided that since so many other "readings" were on target, this "past lives" theory must be valid as well. Not only that, but the spirits also spoke with what seemed like credible authority.

The logic of reincarnation comforted me. It taught that God had created us as perfect beings, but we had each decided at some point to rebel and go our own way. Thus would begin a long series of repeated lifetimes, each of which would give us an opportunity to repay this Supreme Being for our rebellion. Through hardships and interpersonal strife (the result of rebellion), indebtedness to God could be paid back—by our performing well. This belief began to satisfy my "wondering" questions. For instance:

Why is this happening to me?
Why do I have a terrible stepmother?
Why is there suffering?

Reincarnationists take the view that we are to aim for perfection from lessons we learn down here. If we haven't learned all of these lessons before death, then our spirit will need to return in a different body. Multiple incarnations will occur until perfection is achieved, and then we will be allowed to enter into a perfect cosmos in the heavenlies. This became more than a theory to me. It sat well with my logical mind. The payback (Karma) aspect satisfied my desire to see justice done in the universe.

I was the only Jewish person in our "Search for God" group. (Actually that was true of all the unconventional philosophies in which I was a participant.) This brought some uneasy feelings at first, for I was opening my home to Gentiles each week. But since I had no Jewish friends who were "searching" for something more, I decided it was worth the relative discomfort.

Interestingly, the Edgar Cayce books would sometimes quote from the New Testament—using the words of Jesus Christ. A chill of guilt would ripple through me whenever I read his name. For a time I mentally substituted the name "Moses" or "Solomon" for the name "Jesus." I told myself it didn't really matter *who* said something, but only *what* was said. And the words attributed to Jesus Christ, to my surprise, were deeply profound.

My group was immersed in the Cayce study books and practiced specific directives. For example, one week we would focus on a person we resented and apply distinct principles to rid ourselves of bitterness. The next week we might work on a bad habit, like smoking or nail biting. At first we were all excited as we sat in our circle sharing:

"The discipline worked!"

"I didn't lose my temper."

"My mother-in-law and I got along this week."

Each week without fail, several participants would relate paranormal experiences. One woman held up an antique locket and told us about its history and first owner—information she had received from a supernatural source; later she found out the details were correct. Someone else did automatic writing with a spirit guiding her hand. Another group member reported seeing colorful auras around our heads and interpreted the meanings, while someone else had been visited by spirits in ancient costumes.

My wondering as to what else went on outside the material realm didn't end with Cayce . . .

CHAPTER 8

DEEPER AND DEEPER I GO

Aside from my dedication to Edgar Cayce, I'd pay psychics to give me readings. They would tell me flattering things about purported past lives or offer encouraging prophecies of future well-being.

The lure of hypnotism was also strong. I found a Jewish hypnotist in Baltimore who analyzed my handwriting and instructed me on non-physical secrets of the universe. Not wanting to continue the financial outlay, I learned self-hypnotism.

Séances, though enthralling and fascinating, were a bit frightening. We would sit in a circle, where a medium would go into a trance-like state. His voice would change and a spirit, speaking through him, would explain mysteries, purporting to reveal secrets of the unknown. At one meeting, I saw spirits flying around the room.

The medium let us know that the spirits could not break through unless we sang hymns. I was not familiar with Christian hymns, so I just listened. Interestingly, most everyone sitting in the séance had been a churchgoer, and a few were still part of a congregation. The Gentiles felt comfortable with this since hymns were considered "good." The mindset was that if we were singing good and holy hymns, that which followed must be good and holy as well. We considered it marvelous if the spirit-world would deem our group worthy of a visitation. I felt so blessed, so privileged, to be up close and personal with this hidden, spiritually advanced world.

One aspect of all this was a strange and sad thing for me personally: During séances, the spirits would always ignore me but would draw close to everyone else, chatting personally with them and answering questions. I, too, would comment and ask questions but our metaphysical visitors disregarded me. I remember one spirit actually sitting on someone's lap, indicating a real fondness for that person. Yet no spirit ever showed me affection, though I longed for affirmation. This caused me to wrestle with feelings of, *I'm not good enough to deserve their attention. What is wrong with me? Why don't they take to me?*

For me, the inveterate learner, it was natural to have many questions about the invisible world where spirits dwelled. But the supernatural realm appeared to ignore me! For example, when Bernie and I used a Ouija board to get answers, it would tell us nothing. Not only that, but I seemed unable to do transcendental meditation properly. Nor was I successful at contacting spirits, perceiving auras around people, or using mental telepathy or automatic writing.

I was jealous of those who regularly experienced these manifestations. The bottom line: I wasn't much of a psychic success. It was disheartening, after all this time, not to exhibit these supernatural gifts—especially when my friends did. Consequently, I redoubled my efforts by reading more books on the supernatural and parapsychology, and spent more money than others on materials, conference travels, and hiring spiritual "sages."

Where was Bernie during this saga? He was standing on the sidelines. Bernie's only interest in the paranormal surfaced when he accompanied me to my astrologer in order to obtain stock market predictions. After the woman gave information about Wall Street, she surprised me by predicting my father would be dead in a year.

As it turned out, the stock market performed exactly the way she said it would. Bernie knew what to buy and made money, but her accuracy left me waiting month after month for my father to die. Thoughts of his death relentlessly invaded my heart. However, Daddy lived to a ripe old age, and I found myself wrestling with the notion that astrologers were not always trustworthy. How could I discern which information was true or false?

Looking back, I recognize the New Age movement to be the umbrella over *everything* in which I was involved during those years. In fact, what historically might once have been termed Buddhism or Hinduism actually fell in the category of the modern New Age era, which is actually the single biggest religion of all time.

This man-based faith attracted me. It offered a spiritual experience, a salvation of the world, and a universal consciousness that one could tap into. It was devoid of a *personal* Father God, but instead the New Age viewpoint affirmed that God was inside of us, which made us all little gods. Since it was a religion of works and not faith, I could tend to my own soul. It felt so good to accept the fact that I had the power within me to not only save myself but also help solve the problems of the greater community of mankind.

The New Age movement includes various occult groups, mystic religions, witchcraft organizations, pagan religions, ecological organizations, secular organizations and neo-political groups which embrace ideals that run counter to widely known guiding principles. In the United States and Canada, over 10,000 organizations are identified as New Age.

No other religion has risen to notoriety as fast or appeared to accomplish as much as the New Age movement. I was the perfect target for this belief system. There's no doubt that the objective of all my gurus and my study books was to substitute the god of self for the God of the Bible.

No one in the cults I was engaged in ever mentioned the possibility that evil was a part of the activities consuming our days. I never once heard the name "Satan." Why talk about the devil when there is none? He was just a myth. We all had better things to busy ourselves with than mythology. A literal devil? Demonic activity . . . *oh, really*? What foolish *wonderings*—and none that I ever entertained!

CHAPTER 9

HEAVENLY INVASION

One January afternoon, as I was in my bedroom practicing Transcendental Meditation, something happened that was as chilling as the frigid temperature outside. A female spirit audibly, piercingly addressed me with a question. (This was a first for me.) Her voice, which was harsh and ugly, came from outside my body, slightly behind my right shoulder. I believed I was hearing the voice of an angel or a helpful spirit guide.

Why, then, did she sound so shrill, so like a shrew? It was unsettling, to say the least, but I had no "file" in my head labeled "Demonic Activity." I had never learned of demons or hellish visitations. Spirits were always speaking at the séances in charming, easy-to-listen-to angelic tones.

"What can I do for you, honey?" the horrible voice asked. I was startled and frightened, but alarm quickly switched to delight. A spirit was speaking personally *to me!* I answered promptly with something magnanimous like, "I want peace in my heart, in my home, and in the United States of America."

It was, I realized, a bland statement, but my thoughts simply were not focused on how to craft a fitting response. My soaring elation that a personal spirit had, at long last, communicated superseded all else.

The spirit didn't reply, but I wasn't bothered. I couldn't wait to tell my friends I had finally joined their ranks. Now there would be a source of guidance and direction for the remainder of my life. The gurus had taught me that once the spirit world made the initial breakthrough to a person, it would be a regular occurrence.

I decided a short nap was justified after this spectacular happening, after which I'd make some calls to fellow seekers and share my exciting news.

In this good mood, I took a few steps to the bed and lay down on my stomach, a favorite sleeping position. Normally I'd be dead to the world in about five minutes, but this time sleep would not come. I was sharply aware of traffic noise, and the tumbling of the dryer—*Oh dear, I should have taken the permanent press clothes out before I lay down.* I longed for a nap but was, oddly, in a wide-awake state.

Then without warning, from somewhere outside of my body, a burst of power, strong as a tornado, rammed into my body. I should have been killed but felt no pain from the direct hit.

Next, I realized I no longer was in my body. I looked from where I had been thrown outward and upward and saw—through the roof of my home—my body lying on the bed. It was still in the same position. I was on my stomach, arms by my side, my head turned sideways, facing left. Though I was observing myself from above, I knew I was still Judy. I could think and feel and see. I knew I had a body; I had arms and legs. *But where am I?*

Suddenly, a blinding light shone everywhere, removing everything recognizable from my sight. The light threw its mantle over my house below and over everything in the material world. My first thoughts were, *How can I ever describe to anyone the whiteness of this light? No bleached white sheets, no newly fallen snow—nothing I have ever seen—is this white or bright.* It was as blinding as the sun at noon in a cloudless sky.

The next marvel was not for my eyes, but for my ears. Bells, bells and . . . *more* bells. I heard the music of thousands of bells ringing throughout the universe. Huge bells, tiny bells, and chimes of every sort merged into melodious harmony beyond human description. The music was *heavenly*! No earthly bells could have imitated their song. I wanted to hear the joyous music for the rest of eternity.

Then rising out of that symphony came a voice—deep, loud, masculine. He spoke from outside of my soul, or from outside of *wherever* I was at that point. The speaker's words had an authority that struck terror in my heart. Yet I was awed because the sheer volume and timbre of his voice were rich and altogether holy and majestic. I thought I would perish at the glory of it. My whole being was enraptured by its majesty, its resonance.

He spoke many things to me, but out of fear, I kept throwing my hands (albeit spiritual hands) over my ears, shutting out the words. I could not bear the splendor of the man's voice. But I did hear one sentence, spoken with such power that it burned itself into my soul:

"And the Bible says, 'Believe on the Lord Jesus Christ and you will be saved, and your house.'"

Eventually, there was silence. He had ceased speaking to me, the music stopped, and the light disappeared. Then the thought gripped me: *How am I to get back into my body on the bed?* I scrunched my spiritual body tightly by bringing my knees chestward and pushing my elbows against my side, all the while grimacing because I couldn't seem to get anywhere.

I was working hard to pull, to go downward from somewhere up in the universe. Then to my complete surprise, I realized I was back in my physical body.

My first thought was, *I need to tell someone.* I tried reaching for the nightstand phone and was distressed to discover I couldn't move; I was paralyzed. All I could move were my eyelids. I kept blinking, though it mattered not, since my eyesight was gone. I was blind. I knew I was alive; it was just that my physical body was unresponsive to my brain. Gradually—I didn't note the time—the ability to move, and to see, returned sometime that afternoon.

The next few days I walked around in a stupor. Emotionally, I was living half-in, half-out of this world. I felt disconnected from people and my normal routine. I tried to share the experience with Bernie, but my words were sorely lacking; they just couldn't convey the enormity of what had occurred. Neither my husband nor I could make sense of what had occurred.

I am still hampered by the inadequacy of human communication—there is no music, no light, and no voice on earth with which to compare that supernatural experience. Other than Bernie, there was no one I wanted to speak to about the heavenly visitation. How could another human being appreciate my description if he wasn't there? How could I do justice to the magnificence of every facet of the experience? It was absolutely sacred to me. And I was afraid that the totality of what had occurred would somehow be diminished by the telling.

After several days, the mysterious effect of feeling half-in and half-out of this world began to wear off. I was more like myself, yet the longing for the music and the magnificent light lingered.

At the next weekly meeting of the Cayce group, I decided, hesitantly, to share what happened. All listened closely and with great interest, but none could fathom such a thing or know how to respond. One woman suggested it was my master spirit guide who had contacted me. What else could it be?

Eventually, the story was forgotten by the group, by Bernie, and even pretty much by me. Whoever it was who had spoken to me in that thunderous voice was no longer at the forefront of my thoughts. There was so much else going on. Not only was I raising four children, but I was also fully engaged in the New Age movement and its branches.

One morning, weeks after the phenomenon, I received an invitation to go see Betty, a fellow seeker in all things supernatural. She had something to show me. We stood in her kitchen as she removed a plaque from her lavender flowered wallpaper. "Was this what you heard, Judy?" I read the words—"Believe on the Lord Jesus Christ, and thou shalt be saved, and thy house."

Betty told me the plaque quoted a verse from the New Testament. She and I stood in silence, neither one knowing what to say next. I had nothing to offer; neither did she. Betty was a quiet, gentle person, a woman of few words. Now she had none, and I—the talkative one—was also at a loss. I left a few minutes later with no more understanding than when I walked through her kitchen door. What was I to do with this? I'm Jewish. *Jesus Christ?* He's not, and can't ever be, in my world.

Months passed. I was working hard to convince myself our Edgar Cayce group was "growing up." But in reality, we seemed to be "growing down" instead. Were we lying to ourselves? It seemed I was the one actually carrying the others on my shoulders. The teacher in me came forth as an encourager and an interpreter of the paranormal mysteries we were exploring.

As time went on, cracks in our armor were starting to appear. People began to tell of bad and strange goings-on.

We thought we were devoting our energies to things pure and good, so what explanation could there be for such ill effects? One woman reported that her hands wouldn't stop shaking. Another recounted having ever-more-frequent nightmares. A mental breakdown sent another member into an asylum. The topic of suicide came up often for one tormented woman. Instead of good fruit emanating from our disciplines and readings, horrific reports became the norm. *How could this be happening?*

Marriages in the group started crumbling through adultery, depression, and various other causes. Ironically and sadly, Bernie ended up handling the divorces for four of the group's six core families.

I wondered often; only now it was a worrisome and clueless wondering. I questioned myself concerning all I was "about." *Futile, foolish, hollow, ineffective.* These words floated around me, overshadowing hope for a transformed nature. The search was devouring my time, my energy and really—my heart.

CHAPTER 10

A NEW SONG

Life continued. The earlier out-of-body heavenly visitation had almost entirely faded in my thoughts. I kept on as before— weekly Edgar Cayce meetings at home, Wednesday services with spiritists, visits with my psychic and my astrologer, along with the continued practice of Transcendental Meditation. In addition, I was engaging in all sorts of fringe activities that made up life as I knew it then.

About a year after hearing that loud, remarkable voice, I was in the kitchen on a sweltering summer day, rinsing the usual iceberg lettuce for the usual dinner salad. *Who knew from nutrient-packed spinach back then?* A section of non-nutritious, almost white iceberg lettuce was washed daily and served nightly by most Jewish homemakers. *Why?* Because our mothers had all washed non-nutritious, almost white iceberg lettuce daily and served it nightly. Thousand Island dressing accompanied the wedges. I had picked up my mother's habit in Philadelphia and imported it to Baltimore after marrying Bernie.

There was, however, one difference in my ritual: My mother always had the radio tuned to soap operas while washing her lettuce; I always had television on while washing mine. I wanted different background noise, as I considered the soaps a waste of good time. My choice was the "never-know-who's-coming-on" talk shows.

That afternoon I was only half-listening when I heard, "And now, I'd like to welcome to our show . . . Mr. Pat Boone!" My heart leaped. When I was a teenager watching movies and collecting pictures of movie stars, Pat was my idol. I loved his broad smile, clean-cut appearance, smooth baritone voice, brilliant mind (graduated magna cum laude from Columbia University), and trademark white buck shoes. Besides all that, he was a descendant of the legendary pioneer Daniel Boone. I had chosen Pat Boone to be the father of my children, but Shirley, his high school love, got to him first.

Pat still holds *Billboard* magazine's record for being on the charts 220 consecutive weeks with one or more hits. At the time, his records were outsold by only one other single vocalist or recording artist, who was also his good friend—Elvis Presley. Not only did Pat have a legendary career in the music business, but like Elvis, he used it as a springboard for a successful acting career, which included twelve Hollywood films. In addition, he hosted his own television series and was a prolific writer.

Dropping the lettuce in the sink, I immediately dropped on a sofa, afraid to miss a word. The host opened the conversation by commenting on how great Pat looked, and how happy he seemed. *C'mon, when hasn't Pat looked great?*

"Well, you're right, I am happy." Pat responded with his famous smile. "But a few years ago I wasn't happy. Everything was falling apart in my life. My marriage relationship was strained, a two million dollar bank note was due, my career had bottomed out, and the skin on my hands was peeling off from anxiety."

I was stunned. For one thing, I could not believe such awful things had happened to this dreamboat since there had been no report of it—not even rumors—in the magazines or newspapers. I thought, *Pat! I cannot fathom why on earth you would be talking about personal matters on national television!* For us Jewish people, our public image was a primary concern. At the same time, I found I could identify with him. My hopes in life were definitely unraveling as well.

Next I heard, "Pat, what makes you so happy now?"

I'll never forget his reply: "It was when I found a personal relationship with God and with Jesus Christ that my whole life changed."

A thousand lights came on inside me. For the rest of the evening, I thought about what Pat had said. Well, to be honest, I thought about half of it. I still could not get past my deeply ingrained belief that Jesus Christ was only for the Gentiles. Though I had never heard more about Jesus than his name, still I was repelled by the thought of him.

Let me compile a little list—one that's not even inclusive— as to why I was totally resistant. I realize not every Jewish person will agree with my observations, nor am I speaking for anyone but myself. These were just *my* thoughts at that exact time, when I sat down to listen to my favorite star:

1. If there is a personal God, there's only one of him— only one who is Divine. It's blasphemy to consider Father, Son, and Holy Spirit all to be God. The *Shema*, which is the centerpiece prayer of the morning and evening Jewish services, says, "Hear, O Israel: The Lord is our God, the Lord is one" (Deuteronomy 6:4). And this one God revealed himself to only one people: the Israelites, his chosen ones.

2. The Holocaust was perpetrated by Gentiles, who killed two-thirds of the Jewish population living in Europe during the Second World War. Hitler's soldiers wore belt buckles that read, "In God We Trust." I connect Jesus to Hitler because the dictator professed to be a Lutheran, a denomination of the Christian faith.
3. My identity is not that of a sinner, so I don't need someone (Jesus) to be punished or to die for me. The rabbi taught that my true identity is a good one.
4. The Bible means nothing to me. I've never read it. It seems obvious the Bible was written by man.
5. *Jesus Christ* is a curse word among friends and family. The name is used only as a dirty word.
6. Jesus Christ is Mary's son. He couldn't be a Jewish Messiah (whatever that entails) since his mother's name was Mary. The only "Marys" I know are Gentile.
7. I lump together Christian, Hindu, Muslim, Buddhist, Protestant, Catholic, and even the Aborigines (!); they are all part of the "other than Jewish" peoples.
8. Jewish people are intelligent for the most part and highly educated; most have prospered since coming to the United States. Why would I want to be part of a different faith group?
9. Among Jewish people, divorce is rare and alcoholism almost unheard of. Those failings are related to Gentiles. Again, why would I want to be part of a different faith group?
10. I do not want anyone trying to proselytize me.

For those reasons and more, as I replayed the TV interview in my mind, I simply put aside the name *Jesus*, even though he was obviously central to Pat's faith. That particular name was too offensive to me as a Jewish woman. But I'd also heard the entertainer mention God, a familiar word to all Jewish people, even if only attending synagogue a few times a year.

I vaguely recalled the rabbi describing God as a gigantic, almighty being, but he seemed to be far off beyond the atmosphere, way too distant for any of us to know him personally. Maybe Moses knew God back in Bible times. Maybe even my rabbi could know him, but not this homemaker.

Even in our Edgar Cayce group, while we definitely accepted the reality of a supreme force or power, I would never have used the word "personal" to describe how we might relate to something in the category of "deity." The connection we had with this power was more of a technicality, like learning how to tune in to a shortwave radio station. Transcendental Meditation was the means I was using.

During the interview, Pat mentioned a book he had written: *A New Song.* I called a department store right away to purchase it, only to discover it was on back order. Three months later, the book arrived. By this time, the excitement of seeing Pat Boone on television had faded, and I used the book simply as something to do—I had no recollection as to why I'd been motivated to order it in the first place. I sank into our black recliner (with my obligatory chocolate bar) and opened to the introduction about 9 p.m. that evening. The four children were finally asleep; Bernie had left for a basketball game.

As I turned the pages, my Jewish intellect would have normally dismissed any spiritual content written by this Gentile man. My educated mind would have gone into high gear, and I'd have skipped over most of what he wrote. I said to myself, *Don't forget—Pat is not Jewish. Just enjoy his story, but don't get personally involved.*

CHAPTER 11

SOMEBODY TOUCHED ME

In reading the book, I intentionally skipped over Bible verses whenever they appeared, but what I couldn't ignore was Pat Boone's personal story. He had received what I wanted—a new heart, a new spirit. Pat wrote he had been changed by a very real and personal God. At the moment, I was impressed, not with who he was in the world's eyes, but rather, *with what he had spiritually.* Was there a way I might also have Pat's peace and joy alive in me—not for a day, but for all my days?

My intellect was the guardian of how I processed information and ideas. But that night it appeared to doze off, making a way for my heart to respond first. I wasn't choosing to let my heart rule over my head. Judy Reamer, the analyst, wouldn't operate that way. Yes, my mind—my reasoning—was quieted, but not of my own doing, for sure.

Pat's story was provoking me to a holy jealousy. He said he had entered this new way of living through the person of Jesus. Oy vey! Even though what Pat shared was completely foreign to me, and that name known only as a curse word, a hope was pushing through. Untouched parts of my soul were somehow starting to sense that his words were not subjective, but absolute truth.

I was about two-thirds of the way through the book when the words began to blur, since my eyes were filling up. I slipped out of the chair and onto the plush beige carpet. Soon my body was gripped with convulsive sobs. I looked up and cried aloud, "I'm trying to be a good person and I don't know how to do it. If you do exist, God, would you show me how to be free of sin? Oh, God, if you are real, if you are personal, help me!"

All along, my emptiness had been a matter of wanting to be "good" on the inside. Out of helplessness, out of brokenness, out of hopelessness, I was speaking to a God I couldn't see, couldn't hear, and couldn't touch. Besides, was he even there? (During these moments, it escaped me that I *had* heard him speak, *had* seen his glory, and *had* experienced his power when he lifted me from my physical body and set me in a heavenly place a year earlier.)

At the time, there was a hit song titled "Is That All There Is?" recorded by top vocalist Peggy Lee. The lyrics paralleled my sentiments:

> *Is that all there is, is that all there is?*
> *If that's all there is, my friends, then let's keep dancing.*
> *Let's break out the booze and have a ball,*
> *If that's all there is.*

Echoing the singer, I cried out, "Is this all there is? What's the meaning of life? Is there a purpose? I have a successful husband, four adorable children, and a sparkling social life. But what about people in Appalachia? What about people born blind? What about those who have cancer? Is it just luck that I don't? I'm so tired of trying to figure life out. I've endeavored to deal with my faults, my weaknesses, and my humanity through all kinds of spiritual disciplines, I barely get anywhere. It appears senseless to keep this search for significance going! Everything up till now smacks of futility, because I never get the results I diligently seek after. What's wrong with me?"

What came next was a torrent of words—all the refuse within me spilled out. Here I was praying for the first time (to an unknown God, no less), confessing into thin air, not knowing if I was heard. For the very first time in my life, I felt an overwhelming need to humble myself. And it was an act of bowing before a *personal* God. I was convinced that if there *was* a God who cared about me, then he was listening to every heartfelt cry for help. I had never, ever talked to anyone the way I was talking to this almighty person.

I was discovering that the soul was my life center, *not self.* I realized the words were not synonymous. I had been preoccupied with "self" for many years, to the disregard of my soul. Self dealt with my life outside of a relationship with God; the soul was the part of me that was communing with God in these holy moments.

My remorse, my confessions, if you will, were for much more than simply wrong outward behavior. I was acutely aware that I myself had played the part of God from the time I was a child. I wanted to be in control; I didn't want to change; I wanted to be independent. But that actually describes who God is! *He is in control; he doesn't change and he is independent.* I was alienated from God because I wanted to be all those things. I had been living solely through self-effort, self-strength, self-determination, and self-sufficiency— which basically translated into a self-centered life.

The Spirit of God hovered over me and broke through the cement of my soul, exposing me to myself in a most powerful way. The bad news: I was worse than I imagined. The good news: God was much better than I could ever have dreamed. And I was about to discover that he was a God of infinite love.

I am such a pragmatist that a part of me chafed at opening up so completely to an invisible God. Yet I felt compelled to trust I wasn't talking to the wind. I wasn't suicidal; I wasn't having a nervous breakdown. I was miserable for one reason only—the realization that there was an unknown part of me entrapped in sin.

Sin wasn't a word used in conversations I'd ever had or heard. Outside of the holiday Yom Kippur, it seldom occurred in Jewish circles. Yet Pat mentioned the Bible speaks of an innate tendency to sin daily. In fact, he wrote that without God, we are enslaved to sin.

Strangely, I was able to accept that premise as truth and believed sin to be part and parcel of every human life—even though I myself had never read it in a Bible. Why did it make sense to me? Well, I never had to teach my toddlers to lie. They just did it naturally. Why was it easier to be selfish than unselfish? Easier to gossip than not? Easier to complain than not? Easier to cheat on tax reports than not? Easier to disobey parents than not? Easier to lust than not? Easier to be greedy than not?

The more I thought about the human condition, the more I realized the immensity of the struggle to be righteous. *You mean this is the norm, Pat? Woe is me! And all this time I thought I was abnormal, since I'd accepted the belief that man was innately good.*

I continued to weep as I came face to face with rebellion in me. As long as I hadn't accepted the reality of God—and with that reality, the truth of his holiness and perfection—I didn't have to deal with any insurgence within myself. As long as I hadn't given any thought to a sovereign God, I could just live and do whatever I desired, short of breaking the law. I'd been living on my credits and using the currency of past laurels—which all leads towards conceit. But through Pat's book, my eyes were opened, and I became convicted about my rebellious state. I saw it wasn't a matter of my deciding, or anyone else deciding for me, whether I was a good or bad person. The question was, How does God see me?

And on that never-to-be-forgotten night, I did see how my thoughts and actions appeared to a holy God. It wasn't through my mind that I perceived my true state. Intellectually, I wanted to believe I was good at my core, since the rabbi had told me so. If I'd been reading my Jewish Scriptures, I would have caught his error. So the conviction didn't come through the Bible, but through a Gentile celebrity's book. The thought occurred: *Why not try . . . why not try Jesus?* Who he was or what it meant to call on his name—those things I couldn't fully grasp. I simply wanted what Pat found in Jehovah God through Jesus—forgiveness, acceptance, love, strength, comfort, peace, deliverance, and an eternity that was beyond description in its beauty.

If Pat had written to call on Donald Duck or told me to eat a Hershey Bar to receive the peace he had, I would have. I trusted that Pat was living proof there was hope, there was something or *somebody* who could make all the difference in life lived on earth . . . and in the hereafter. There's truth in the saying that when you find out someone can hurt you *or help you*, you become mindful of that person. Pat Boone was saying that Jesus, whose followers knew him to be the Jewish Messiah, could change me.

What harm could there be in calling out the name? Would God give me a new heart—a new birth, as it were—through what Jesus did over 2,000 years ago . . . as Pat wrote in his book? I'd expended almost all my strength in crying long and hard, but with one last surge of energy, I allowed the forbidden name to cross my lips. "If *Jesus* is the answer, I want him!"

After that outburst—a faith outburst—I fell silent. The tears stopped completely. A strange composure came over me. My heart, which moments before had been overwhelmingly burdened, was now light. A comfort and joy that I could not explain began to fill me. *What was happening?* It was as though I had been touched by an unseen hand. I was swallowed up in stillness. My winter of discontent had turned into wonderful solace. And all I had done, in complete helplessness, was to come like a little child and cry out, "Jesus!"

Have you ever experienced something amazingly profound yet found yourself unable to clearly express the depth of it? And when you tried to describe it, did you sense that in the telling, something was lost? I knew I couldn't declare rationally what had happened to me. It was more an experiential kind of knowing than intellectual. My heart—my soul—knew it, and nothing could take this "knowing" away. I had had the exact same experience after I'd been returned to my physical body many months ago after hearing the music, seeing the light and hearing God's voice. Words were just inadequate to paint that picture. Same for this evening which will be written always on my heart: Someone had touched me and made me whole.

I was determined that nobody, not even Bernie, would ever find out that I—a Jew—had used the name Jesus in prayer. I'd certainly never tell! With a peace I'd never tasted before, I rose from the floor, sat down again in the recliner—but not as the same person—and finished the book. I knew Bernie would be home soon. I got up to grab a tissue. How ever would I explain "my face," my red eyes to my husband?

As I was standing by the doorway to the kitchen, wiping away the streaked mascara, I began to talk to a God I knew was there. Yet being such a novice at trusting him, I prayed a bit hesitantly. I was afraid to go *all the way* with this newly given faith, so my words sounded tinged with doubt: "Dear

God, *if you are really there and listening,* I would like to write Pat Boone. I don't know where he lives. I would like to thank him. Does he live in Hollywood? He's a movie star. Does he live in New York? Maybe, *if there is a God,* in my *Good Housekeeping* magazine there will be a picture of Shirley and Pat by a pool. The caption could say, 'Pat and Shirley Boone by their pool in Beverly Hills.' Then, *if there is a God,* I could just write a note addressed to Pat Boone, Beverly Hills, California. Certainly the postman will know where Pat lives."

At that point, I heard the key turn in the door and Bernie walked in. But for some reason he just walked over, lightly kissed my lips, and looking straight at me, talked about the basketball game and friends he saw there. My normally inquisitive attorney husband did not notice that anything was different—not even my swollen eyes or smudgy appearance. The only wondering I did this evening was to question why Bernie never asked, "Have you been crying?" What could I have told him anyway? Intellectually, I comprehended *nothing* of what had occurred. As Blaise Pascal wisely wrote, "The heart has reasons that reason does not understand"

And God had reasons to transport me to Sin City a few days later . . .

CHAPTER 12

THE RELUCTANT VACATIONER

The following few days were a frenzy—centered on vacation preparations. In the busyness, Pat Boone's book was forgotten and put aside. There was not a moment to rest, relax, or reflect. I was packing for Bernie and me, writing instructions for Essie, our long-time, dearly loved housekeeper, and shopping for food, diapers, and some new playthings to leave for four tykes. These time-consuming activities stole my focus from the awesome experience three days prior.

We were to accompany Bernie's college roommate Jimmy and his wife Rozzie to Las Vegas. I can't count the number of times I tried to get Bernie to change the plans. "Please, Bernie! Anywhere but Las Vegas!"

It was the last place I wanted to vacation, but he had given his word to our friends, who wanted to experience that notorious town. After all the years I'd given to disciplines and studies to become a better person, I was afraid Las

Vegas—"Sin City"—would be pulling me backwards. I didn't need the temptations I knew would be awaiting me.

Though still resistant, I found myself in the lobby of Caesar's Palace Hotel a couple days later. Before going to check us in, Bernie handed me a brochure and sat me down on a plush sofa. I was an absolutely unhappy camper in an absolutely ritzy camp.

"Here's a list of the performers who are in town this week," he told me. "You choose the ones we should see."

"I don't *want* to see any shows. I want to stay in the room."

"Well, then pick out shows for the rest of us to see."

Bernie and the other two left me with six pieces of luggage and the glossy colored pamphlet. Reluctantly, I opened it and began to scan the list. All the biggest stars seemed to be in town that very week, and the last name on the roster was . . . Pat Boone!

What? my mind shouted. *Pat Boone? This can't be! My eyes are deceiving me!* Stunned, I read his name over and over and over. It was too remarkable to fathom and caught me totally unaware.

Is God involved in this unexpected news? No. Yes. Maybe. I don't know. Is God so real, so personal? Does he care for me like this? Isn't he busy with people who are suffering in prison or in hospitals? I am rich in health, worldly goods, and reputation. Why would he answer my small request when I have everything?

Or is this merely a coincidence? No. Yes. Maybe. Yet, I did ask God to let me know where to find Pat so I could pen a short note. What in the world am I to do with this information? Is Pat Boone here because I am here?

As quickly as those words flooded my mind, they were overshadowed by these accusations: "You ridiculous, highly imaginative, emotional woman! Such conceit. Now, just drop these silly thoughts of a personal God who cares about you enough to arrange such a meeting."

Not only had I doubted *God's* existence in the past; I doubly doubted the existence of a devil. Absurd consideration! A myth! I'd written earlier that I'd never heard Satan mentioned in any of my cultish activities—not once. Yet in hindsight, I now know he directed all of it. Here's an analogy: When I attend the theater with a friend, I have no inkling who occupies the seat on the other side of me. That person may very well be the acclaimed show's director. Sitting there—"hidden" in plain sight—he would remain unnoticed not only by me, but by the rest of the audience; we would recognize and applaud only the stars onstage. I'd be totally consumed with the captivating production—I wouldn't be aware of or care about the unknown person on my left, let alone give him any credit. Yet without the director, the production would never be a success.

At the time, I had no name or category for my disparaging accuser. The "director's" words—"You ridiculous, highly imaginative, emotional woman . . . !"—made more sense to me than God's did. The Lord's encouraging impressions were still too new and unfamiliar to believe. So I fell in with the adversary's words that bombarded me: "Reject any thought that you and Pat Boone were meant to meet. Such a crazy thought!"

"Judy, who's in town this week?" Bernie's voice broke through my thoughts.

Roz added, "We're all checked in. What shows should we book reservations for? You're the expert."

I proceeded to read aloud from the brochure. They were smiling and happy to put out big bucks for any of the stars. Then, rather timidly, I added,

"And Pat Boone is here too. He's at the Fremont Hotel."

"Pat Boone?" Roz answered. "I'd prefer to see the other stars first."

At that point, I was absolutely willing to let go of any ridiculous notion that this entertainer was here for my benefit. But then, unexpectedly, Bernie spoke up.

"Didn't I see a book by him on the table the other day? Did you read it, honey?"

"Well, I actually just finished it."

"Why don't you call Pat Boone and tell him you read his book?"

I stared at Bernie, my eternally sane husband. *What was that he asked?*

"Bernie! Thousands upon thousands have read Pat's book. Why on earth would he care if I read it?"

Then incredibly, Roz (quiet, conservative Rozzie) picked up on Bernie's suggestion.

"I dare you to call him, Judy!"

"No! I can't! I won't!"

Level-headed Jimmy chimed in. "Chicken! You're just a chicken!"

"Stop it, Jimmy!"

What was wrong with these people? In all our times together, I was always the teaser and they were my audience. The trio weren't acting like themselves. Bernie was a quiet, gentle, laid-back and conservative man. I had never known him to command, shove, push, or cajole me into anything. Jimmy and Rozzie were shy and bashful people. In fact, I was the only outgoing person of the foursome. (All three of them used to say I was the only one who had any personality!)

Now our roles had become oddly reversed. We stood by the luggage and the plush furniture, going back and forth with their goading and my refusing. I was really annoyed with Bernie for making a scene in the lobby. "Stop this," I protested. "We've flown five hours. I want to go to the room! I'm tired and want to shower." But they were relentless, so I tried a different tactic: "Let's go see what our room is like, and I'll call Pat Boone from there." (I had no intention of doing any such thing; I planned only to berate Bernie for pushing me to do something I'd made perfectly clear I didn't want to do.)

And now they began to fire in rapid succession.

"Oh, call Pat Boone already!"

"What's the big deal?" "Did you like his book?"

"Well, call him and tell him."

"I dare you."

"You've never been a chicken before."

"What's your problem?"

"All of a sudden you're getting shy on us?"

Then my husband declared, "Judy, we're not going to the room until you call Pat Boone."

I was so upset with this man! Who was this stranger? Bernie was not himself! Come to think it, Jimmy and Roz weren't exactly themselves either.

The Three Musketeers (swords drawn) pretty much pushed me over to a phone in the corner of the lobby. Bernie dialed the Fremont Hotel and handed over the receiver. The nerve of him! How I wound up with the phone in my hand, I don't know. I heard a voice: "Fremont Hotel. May I help you?" The woman repeated, "Fremont Hotel. May I help you?"

I uttered abruptly, "Operator, is Pat Boone there, please?"

"No, Mr. Boone is not in at this time."

Again came the accusing "director's" voice. "Now Judy, if this was indeed of God, after you went to the trouble of calling, he would have made sure Pat Boone was there. The options have now disappeared. There is no Pat Boone for you. Hang up the phone!"

I was about to submit to this voice that I had always obeyed. The enemy of my soul usually made sense to me, or I wouldn't have followed his suggestions. *So hang up, Jude.* (That's my name when I'm having conversations with myself.) *Forget about it, Jude.* Then to my surprise, an unlikely idea popped up from somewhere *new* in me—*Tell the operator to have Pat Boone call you.*

I heard myself say, "Please ask Mr. Boone to call Judy Reamer between 5:00 and 6:30 tonight at Caesar's Palace." I slowly set the phone back on the hook. I felt ridiculous and nervy. How could I have ever asked him to return my call? Besides, I gave him only an hour and a half in a twenty-four hour day to get in touch with—Judy Reamer? Who's she, anyway? Certainly that would be the thought of a celebrity who got pestered by a fan's phone call.

CHAPTER 13

AN UNLIKELY PHONE CALL

Finally in our room by mid-morning, we unpacked and changed clothes. The four of us spent the rest of the day orienting ourselves to the monstrous hotel and visiting the nearby—also monstrous—Hoover Dam. About 5 p.m. we rushed back to dress for dinner, which for me was quite a process.

An hour later I stood at the bathroom mirror, bright pink lipstick in hand for a reapplication. Next, I checked to see if any hairs were out of place, which was highly unlikely since my coif had been lacquered with hairspray. Though popular at the time, I now realize my hairdo looked less like my own hair than it did a bad wig. My small face was framed with the "tease fluff" style. To accomplish this, I had to take one small portion of hair at a time and hold it straight up in the air with one hand; then, holding a narrow-tooth comb in the other hand, I'd backcomb (tease) the hair until it stood up on its own.

My medium-length hair took fifteen minutes to "tease," at which point one might have guessed I'd touched my forefinger to an electrical outlet. Once the hair was standing at attention, I used a hair-pick to smooth the ends into a shape resembling a huge helmet. Bernie was never able to run his fingers through my hair. And all night I looked like a mummy, since I would sleep with toilet paper wrapped around "the do" to keep its shape. Adding icing to the cake, my light brown hair was frosted with a golden shine that rivaled my glistening brass Passover menorah.

My formal attire for the evening was a yellow, silver, and gold, fully sequined, tight, mini-skirted cocktail dress. I looked as if I'd been chosen to play the sun in a third-grade play. Completing my outfit were silver fishnet chorus-girl hosiery (fitting for a cancan girl in Paris's Moulin Rouge nightclub) and yellow stiletto heels. I was dressed to the hilt.

And jewelry? Funny you should ask. My stepfather was in that business, so I was the proud owner of a long chain necklace attached to three gold discs that gonged as I walked. When my heavy solid gold charm bracelet would accidentally hit my necklace, people would get up from their seats, go into the dining room and ask, "Where's dinner?" Then there was my pinkie ring. Its large stone looked as if someone had extracted the bauble from the diamond mines and forgotten to cut it into five smaller stones.

To complete the picture, my pricey perfume was certain to smack people in the face, leaving them reeling as it wafted off my person. To put it mildly, I was Webster's definition of *overkill*.

As I stood at the mirror putting on "finishing touches," the hotel phone sounded with a harsh, grating tone. Bernie picked it up before the third ring. "Judy, it's Pat Boone!"

Well, I wasn't born yesterday. I took the phone from Bernie and answered, "Hello" with an annoyed, flippant tone. It was Jimmy on the other end of the line. *Or was it?* If it *was* Jimmy, he was doing a phenomenal imitation of Pat's mellow, clear voice. I knew Pat's voice as a singer, and knew his speaking voice well from movies. I even knew his signature shoes—white bucks.

"Hi Judy, this is Pat. Pat Boone."

I slowly sat down on the bed. It wasn't Jimmy. It was *him*, my heart-throb. I took a deep breath. What words to speak? This moment wasn't in the plan!

"Pat, I'm a Jewish girl from Baltimore. I just read your book. I only called to thank you for your willingness to be transparent. Thank you so much for writing it." And then I didn't know what else to say, so I wanted to hang up. What does a woman say to her teenage idol, to a Hollywood legend? How could I dare ask, "Would you please sing me a few bars of 'April Love' or 'Love Letters in the Sand' or 'Ain't That a Shame?' or anything you feel like warbling?"

"Judy, please come see me after my show tonight. Bring your husband too."

Somehow, before hanging up, I got out an "Okay, thank you."

I was staring at Bernie, not believing what had just happened. I told him of Pat's request: "He wants to meet both of us."

My husband was very calm, unlike excited me. "We'll catch Pat's late show," he said. "After that, I'll take you up to his dressing room, and I'll wait in the casino for you." (Bernie had no interest in anything "Hollywood.")

I was relieved by his disinterest. I had kept quiet about my turning to God a few nights earlier. Bernie was never to know I had taken the name of Jesus seriously, rather than as the curse word we often heard. I had a foreboding that if my husband joined me in the star's dressing room and the conversation took a spiritual turn, Pat Boone might speak of Jesus—to both of us! Additionally, what if he took out a Bible and began reading from the New Testament? And what if, and what if, and what if . . . ?

After the dinner show with our Annapolis friends, Bernie and I took a cab to the Fremont Hotel. Following Pat Boone's marvelous performance, my husband escorted me up the stairs to Pat's dressing room, with no intention of joining me inside.

It took two knocks for the door to open. Pat, still wearing his white tuxedo show attire, opened the door and shook Bernie's hand. To his surprise, Pat's strong handshake, as well as the star's gracious, welcoming words, were enough to result in us *both* entering the spacious dressing room. To his credit, Pat didn't wince as his eyes rested on me, for I was a dazzling, sparkling sight to behold. He never let on that I looked absolutely ridiculous! *I* still wince as I recall my appearance! I guess Pat was accustomed to "over the top" people. After all, I pretty much was imitating the current Hollywood fashion.

"Please sit down. I'll be right out after I change." Bernie, being a polite man (and also not wanting to admit he'd rather gamble than be there), sat down slowly on a soft-cushioned loveseat. I could tell he was clueless as to how he wound up sitting on the couch rather than on a stool at a Black Jack table downstairs. He wasn't enjoying that sofa any more than I had enjoyed the sofa in Caesar's lobby that very morning—but that was before I read the flyer with the lineup of performers.

Sporting a colorfully striped shirt and tan slacks, Pat came back into the room, minus the performance attire and stage make-up. This Hollywood legend was known to be a snappy dresser. His white shoes had been exchanged for a pair of short, polished brown boots. I was puzzled to see a gold Jewish star hanging on his neck. What was that about?

From the start of our visit, I could sense he was a man who loved people. His natural charm was obviously authentic. Pat told us that for the past fifteen years he had been booked into the Fremont the same week every year. This year, for some reason, his agent changed the booking. *That's amazing, I thought. The agent changed Pat's regular week to the week we would be here? Is it coincidental or God's fault? Is God really this personal? Did God have a plan and arrange all this, in spite of my kicking (for months) against coming to Sin City? No. Yes. Well . . . maybe. I can't be sure.* These were dizzying thoughts.

"Pat, you're such a busy man. How is it you returned my call? I left no room number, no message, and only gave you a small window of time to reach me."

"Well Judy, I don't return calls, other than to family and friends. I travel around the world, and when I get back to my hotel, the operator always has a long list of calls waiting. I get calls from fans wanting to meet me, from organizations asking me to speak, from business partners and the like. I had returned this afternoon from a drive out to the mountains where I had gone to pray. When I read the list of calls, your name leaped off the paper. I just knew I was to call Judy Reamer. I don't know why. I never do that with an unknown caller."

I had no words. Inwardly though, I questioned, *What does all this mean?* Once again, I found myself a bit off balance; the implications of Pat's story were jarring. I shifted in my chair and deliberately shifted the conversation. Knowing this was my one and only chance to put Pat Boone on the spot with all my doubts and questions about God, I told myself, *Okay, Jude, forget about Bernie. Ask Pat everything you want, and don't worry—you'll save your marriage later.*

An endless stream of questions rose up from within me. I began to powerfully fire every Jewish argument I could think of at this calm and gracious man. My aim was to refute everything pertaining to Jesus being the Messiah. All I had been taught, all the assumptions I had made, and every conclusion I had reached pressed forward with force.

Right up until recently, I had completely rejected all claims of Christianity. The easiest way to explain would be to mention my yellow, size medium, Playtex rubber gloves. I wear them when washing dishes. Always have and always will. Why? Because my mother wore yellow, size medium, Playtex rubber gloves. How many of my strongly held convictions were truly my own, and how many had I inherited? I was beginning to see I had always rejected the claims of Christianity—and any other religion—because my family, rabbi, and peers did. The way they automatically accepted the "correct" Jewish viewpoint made me assume I had no right to delve into such weighty matters. After all, I was no expert. Who did I think I was to question the authorities?

I was pretty surprised that I would even consider putting myself in the same room with a Christian stranger who would endeavor to say more than two words about his faith. I had always been very suspicious (and downright insulted) if someone even made a veiled attempt to try and convince me Christianity was valid for a Jewish person.

None of my searing questions appeared to upset Pat. On the contrary, he seemed at ease answering whatever I asked. At some point, Pat stood up and reached for a Bible (which I hadn't noticed was sitting a few feet away from the stash of stage make-up). I glanced at my husband, but he remained oddly silent. Where was Bernie the attorney—the man who only hours earlier in the lobby had been so very animated?

With Bible open, Pat Boone poured through the Hebrew Scriptures, showing me the prophecies about a coming Messiah from the line of David, from the tribe of Judah. *I had already made it clear from the start that the New Testament was off limits.* "The New Testament is something we Jewish people never read. I'm fully Jewish, Pat. I love my Jewish culture." (The saying kept coming to mind: "You can take the boy out of the country, but you can't take the country out of the boy.")

To my delight and relief, Pat smiled and was genuinely thrilled that I treasured my culture. "I love your heritage, Judy." (Ah, that explains the Jewish star on his neck.) "The nation of Israel stands as a testament to a miracle-working God. You were born to a Jewish family . . . and so was Jesus."

What did Pat just say? I'm certain he's mistaken. Jesus was a "goy." Don't try to sell me on a Jewish Jesus! He was Gentile and belongs with the Gentiles. Period!

"Well, if Jesus was born to an Israelite mother, when did he abandon his Hebrew religion and start a brand new Gentile religion?"

"He never did, Judy. There was no such religion back then as Christianity. It's not mentioned in the New Testament, which is the story of the birth and death of this Israelite, Jesus. It may help you to know that *Christ* is the Greek way of saying 'Messiah.' The word *Christ* is *not* a Gentile word." (That fact was of great interest to me.)

"The original bearers of the message were Israelites, as were all the early followers. Thousands of them. Eventually, because they were followers of Jesus (the) Christ—i.e., Messiah—they became known as *Christians.* Israel was chosen as the nation to bring forth the Messiah, to bring good news first to the Israelites and then to the other peoples of the world. God kept other nations from destroying Israel, since the Messiah had to come from its loins. The Christ— the Savior—had to be a descendent of Abraham, Isaac, and Jacob."

The drab green-and-taupe dressing room felt brighter. The dynamic conversation was bringing the room alive. I needed to be still for a couple of minutes in order to let Pat's words settle in. My eyes remained fastened on him. I thought, *My being Jewish is not a problem then? Jesus was a*

Hebrew, as was his mother Mary. The Messiah's mother had to come from the line of King David, according to Messianic prophecy.

Until this midnight hour, I had known nothing of the Messianic promises. That this crucified Jesus had his foundation in my Hebrew Scriptures was especially troubling. *Why?* Because I thought the death of Jesus on a cross was solely the concern of everyone that was *other* than Jewish, *other* than an Israelite, *other* than of Hebraic background; I had pictured Jesus as belonging to anyone *but* Israel's forefathers. But now *I* wanted to know: *What had he done to justify his terrible death?*

CHAPTER 14

ONE "AHA" AFTER ANOTHER . . .

"Judy, when you do read the entire New Testament for yourself, you will find no fault in Jesus. He did nothing wrong, was good to everyone with needs, healed the sick, the blind, the deaf, the lame, and set free demon-possessed people. His touch and his words produced miracle upon miracle. But he *did* verbally attack the religious leaders, the self-righteous Pharisees, for their pride, greed, and unloving treatment of the common people. And what perturbed the Pharisees most was that Jesus told them he was the Promised One of their Holy Writ. They falsely believed that performance (keeping the Mosaic Law) was how they could obtain righteousness in God's sight. Jesus was offering them a righteousness that would come through faith—faith in him.

"Jesus came from the Father and had always been with Him. So by living among the first-century Jews, he "put a face" on their idea of God, thereby enabling them to understand more about the Father. "You'll be reading about the fulfillment of the Messianic prophecies. You'll see the details of God's amazing gift of grace—the forgiveness and joy given to those who put their trust in the Messiah. You became a recipient a few nights ago in Baltimore, but the understanding of the goodness and the love of a perfect God will go deeper and wider."

I became silent again . . . and pondered. Each time Pat gave me additional information, I felt the need to get quiet in order to formulate more questions or craft more comments. As I deliberated, my eyes danced all around the room since I mused better that way. There were six pen and ink drawings above the mirrors behind Pat. The Grand Canyon, Hoover Dam, and other iconic Western pictures were hung in an engaging arrangement by someone who knew how to display pictures. I'd usually notice that kind of thing because of my art background. Pat sat quietly, too, since he sensed I was thinking—thinking hard, thinking deeply.

It struck me that rather than being the enemy of Judaism, Christianity was actually its completion. An analogy pushed its way forward in my thoughts: Just as a mystery novel is incomplete without the concluding chapters, in the same way, God's perfect plan for His creation is incomplete without the "last chapters"—that is, the New Testament, which is also called the New Covenant.

"I'd always been taught there were two Bibles, one for the Gentiles and one for the Jewish people."

"Not so." explained Pat, "It's one Bible made of the Old— or First—Covenant and the New Covenant, which contains the perfect conclusion to the Messianic prophecies you never saw or studied."

I again got quiet, turning my face upward to the ceiling from which hung a bright brass light fixture, along with some recessed spot lighting. As I gazed on high for a few moments, I was processing these new ideas: *The New Testament—it's a historic story, which is the completion of the prophets' writings. Hmmm.*

I leaned back on the green suede side chair for a couple more minutes and then commented, "So, Pat, you are saying that when the Hebrew Scriptures closed, the reader was left hanging, right? And in a sense, the Jewish Writ seems to be a 'who-done-it' book. The reader is left with unfulfilled Messianic promises. What you're saying is that there's some mystery involved with the Hebrew Scriptures. The historic accounts in the New Covenant give the solutions to the clues left in the First Covenant, correct?"

I sat up straight now, waiting for Pat, who shifted in a leather swivel chair where his make-up had been applied hours earlier. The chair didn't appear comfortable. I felt bad but sensed he cared about his guests' comfort, not his own. Bernie was still sitting silently on the most comfy piece of furniture in the room—the wide-striped satin loveseat. Pat's concern was only to listen well to my questions and comments, and to give me clear, simple answers.

"Yes, it's one amazing story, and when you close the cover, the dots all connect. The entire New Covenant points back to the Hebrew Scriptures, just as the Hebrew Scriptures point forward to the New Covenant. The words were written by Israelites, just as they were in the Old Covenant."

Hour upon hour we talked. We continued to look through the best-selling book of all time, through many of the familiar Bible stories, but now these stories took on new meaning. I began to understand the significance of the Jewish rituals, the sacrifices, and the laws. The problem had been that though God was in the Israelites' *lives*, in most cases he was not central to their *hearts*. This turning away from God left the chosen nation looking for significance, adequacy, direction, comfort, peace, and love amongst themselves, or within themselves. Just as I had done my whole life! God was wonderfully holy and glorious, reaching out to give them all they needed, but they wanted to be in control of their own existence.

Throughout the night, questions kept pouring out of my head, or was it my heart? Pat remained humble, joyful, and gracious . . . never once interrupting me. He answered every question with a Bible passage or verse, then proceeded to relate personal life applications to help me gain an understanding of God in the here and now.

Just what if . . . yes, Jude, just what if . . . the claims of Christianity are true? My head was now fully engaged, but it was more than just an intellectual perception. A few nights earlier, the fullness of God had swept into my heart, but now my mind, my intellect, was becoming engaged spiritually. The experience I had at home—of surrendering to God, of desiring to know Jesus (though I knew nothing except the name)—was being providentially confirmed. This worldwide entertainer was giving *rational* confirmation to my *experiential* newfound freedom.

At the close of this "night of nights," I was convinced by Scripture that the ancient seers like Isaiah, Ezekiel, Jeremiah, and even the psalmist King David, had foretold the day when a man would be born to undergo great suffering for fallen humanity. In this terrible sacrifice, made by God himself, would be the way that I could have a new spirit, a new heart. A great Christmas gift for a Chanukah girl!

Pat wheeled his chair over to me. I leaned forward one more time to look with him at the verses pointing to all of mankind being *born with depravity reigning in the soul.* Pat was showing me the remedy in the Bible—the way to be changed within. Yes, a few nights before, I had truly experienced the reality of that remedy: "Believe on the Lord Jesus Christ and you will be saved." And now I was seeing that very verse in Scripture—the same words I had heard from the remarkable Voice. Now, for the first time, my eyes feasted on these words *in the Bible.* (The Book of Acts, chapter 16, verse 31 in the New Covenant.)

Despite having been taught I was basically good at my core, the years of encountering my own selfish nature caused me to now accept what the book on Pat's lap spoke of: My heart was depraved in God's sight, and I therefore needed the Savior, the Messiah. New heart, new Judy!

Pat spoke to me about the fact that God is not mocked, no matter what people believe about Him.

"The Lord is aware of our deepest thoughts, Judy."

"Pat, it's been easy for me to put on a false face with others and even fool myself, but I'm learning, through you, that God is aware of our motivations to appear better than we are. I get it. God knows not only our thoughts and feelings, but our motives too. What's so neat is that I'm learning about *God's* thoughts, feelings, and motivations. And they're all perfect!"

I had seen God's blazing glory a year earlier and had heard His wondrous voice and the magnificent music of heaven. But now that I was finally armed with some biblical understanding, I truly desired him to be central in my life. I told Pat this and then glanced at my watch. It was 4:15 a.m.! Pat's eyes were bloodshot, and I doubt my appearance was any better.

I looked at Bernie, who was still very much awake. How on earth had he kept silent all this time? It was as if God had strapped a Band-Aid across his mouth. *A miracle?* I remembered something from Sunday school about Daniel in the lions' den: The mouths of those fierce animals were sealed supernaturally. I said to myself, *God can shut mouths. Look at Bernie!*

There was still one lingering question. "Pat, in your book, you wrote about baptism. That brings to mind an ancient

Jewish rite symbolizing spiritual cleansing. It was about repentance and getting right with God. Is that what baptism represents?"

"That is very much the core meaning of being baptized."

So I drew a deep breath, "If you are willing, Pat, I'd like you to baptize me."

"I'd love to. I'll pick you up at 4 p.m. tomorrow at your hotel."

I looked toward my husband, desperately hoping for a hint of his approval. My thought was, *Bernie, speak now or forever hold your peace.* And astoundingly, he held his peace. In fact, the only words I heard him utter during the entire visit were, "Nice to meet you, Pat" and now—"Good-night, Pat."

CHAPTER 15

LAUGHTER AND TEARS

A revolving door emptied into the lobby of Caesar's Palace, depositing quite a collection of persons. The "people watchers" (and do we know anyone who isn't?) could sit for hours admiring, or marveling at, the interesting sights.

At 4 p.m., just twelve hours after the Bible had come alive to me, all the "people watchers" were rewarded when Pat Boone emerged from the moving doors into the plush Greek-themed lobby. He quickly walked over to where I was seated, offering a hug and a big smile before escorting me out. *Who is this woman strolling out on the arm of Pat Boone?*

Though in the past my smiles would have come from the attention of a celebrity (as editor-in-chief in high school, I'd interviewed several), now my wide grin came from a heart fully aware of God's merciful and loving attention. My soul was singing for joy because the Lord had wooed me to himself!

As Pat drove, he told me he'd contacted a number of friends about the possibility of using their swimming pool for the water baptism—the stars' names were household words. But nothing panned out for that afternoon. Pat had wanted to baptize me in a private pool because, as he said, "You are not getting baptized to receive a Catholic, Episcopalian, Baptist, or any other denominational identity. This baptism is unto the Jewish Messiah. This is not about church affiliation, but about a very real and personal relationship with God."

"Pat, I feel as if I'm about to be married. I'm as excited as a bride would be."

This new friend began to wipe tears from his eyes. "You *are* going to be married."

"What do you mean by that?"

Pat explained, "In a sense, we *are* on our way to your marriage ceremony. You'll publically be declaring your love for God, no longer tied, no longer betrothed, to the false gods of this world. You had been married to the world's ways and have died to those things that ruled your heart, and now you are free to trust God for His perfect purposes for your life. Your life makes sense now; you will have wisdom and understanding as to why you were created. You'll be glorifying and worshiping God with your life. You know He does have a plan for you, don't you?"

Now *my* eyes began to tear up. "When I was a teenager, along with millions of other female fans, I would have married you if I had the chance. What a long way I've come to now wanting to be the bride of the Messiah! That's in a deeply spiritual sense, of course, but this is where real living begins, doesn't it? It's a reality, isn't it?"

Pat nodded and wiped his eyes again, since he couldn't speak. The ride continued as we each reflected silently on the import of that profound conversation.

Our destination, the alternative to a friend's pool, was a church. Pat had called the pastor, who, upon our arrival, welcomed us into his office. The two gracious men spoke with me, answering any remaining questions I had. My immersion was going to signify my belief that my Jewish religion and the prophecies of the Hebrew Bible had their fulfillment in the New Testament narrative.

It was time for "the wedding." Pat showed me to a small room, asked me to don a long cottony, robe-like garment and pointed to some stairs that I was to ascend—and then he left me alone. I was seized with a bit of alarm as a tremendous struggle arose within me. My eyes were fastened on what resembled a hospital gown. *What am I doing? Have I lost my mind?*

There was an exit door in the room. I opened it to find a large boulevard facing me. Lots of taxis were speeding by. *Judy, get out of here! Run as fast as you can. Here you are, getting ready to disrobe to put on a "strange wedding gown"—with none other than Pat Boone waiting for you.* Trivial thoughts began to explode. *What do I take off? What do I leave on? Whatever I leave on will soon be soaked! My hair will be dripping wet, my make-up ruined. Run back to Bernie!*

What kept me from bursting out the exit door and hailing a cab like a runaway bride? Simply, *love*—an almost tangible type I'd never encountered before. Here it was, manifested in the first Christian I had ever come to know. I recognized, from a new place within me, a joy, a peace, and a love shining through Pat's persona. This was nothing less than the goodness of an amazing God who could be "tasted" and "seen" through people who loved Him well. *And* this amazing God could be known through the book Pat showed me last night; a book that had sold over six billion copies—the Bible.

I turned my back on the exit door, removed my shoes and outer garments, pulled the white baptismal gown over my head, and walked up the steps where Pat was waiting. To grasp that it had been only a few nights earlier at home when I'd fallen to my knees in tears . . . and now this.

I didn't know what to expect, but surely not a pool inside a church building! As I surveyed the scene, I felt a bit foolish yet again. The whole situation was surreal. Picture me clad in a white gown, with this famous star standing before me in chest-high, olive green rubber waders. I had never seen fishing boots in my life. He looked rather ridiculous, and I laughed at the sight of him. Here I was, laughing during these sacred moments—and mentally scolding myself: *Judy, how could you?* But it was obvious Pat understood my nervousness, and he laughed with me.

Then, as soon as Pat took my hand and led me into the water with him, the presence of God quieted my heart, and I knew with all my being why I was there.

Pat spoke. "I have only one question, Judy. Do you believe that Jesus is the Son of God, the promised Messiah?"

Time stood still. Then I answered softly with certainty. "Yes, I know this to be true."

He slowly lowered me into the water. "I baptize you in the name of the Father, the Son, and the Holy Spirit."

Then he gently pulled me up. I was laughing and crying. Pat and I were hugging, glorying in the holiness of the moment. I knew who I was now—a forgiven, accepted, unconditionally loved child of God. Furthermore, until this moment, I had never considered the hereafter, but now I understood there *was* an eternity to face. It was pivotal to know where I would be forever. Heaven was no longer a cliché.

Pat and I left the church, lost in our own thoughts. Mine were enveloped in an inexpressible peace. I knew all this had come about by God's intricate design. When Pat took me back to Caesar's Palace and parked the car, I had one more question. It was about someone who was referred to in his book: the Holy Spirit of God, someone of whom I had never heard.

Pat took a few minutes to describe the indwelling of this third Person of the Godhead. I asked him to pray with me regarding the Holy Spirit. I wanted God to gift me in any way he desired so my life could shine for him. All was calm, all was bright. A heavenly tranquility cloaked me. The presence of God's Holy Spirit—I was never to wonder again about him.

CHAPTER 16

CHANGED!

Before Pat drove away, he extended an open invitation to call him at any time. The sun had gone down behind the mountains encircling the small city of Las Vegas. Pat had to get back for two performances that evening, and I also was on a tight schedule—I was supposed to meet Bernie, Roz, and Jimmy at the Sahara Hotel for a dinner show. My dripping wet hair was now flat, with no "fluff" left (Pat commented, "Your "fluff" has "flopped"!); my ruined make-up had painted my face with a vampire look. I rushed back to my room. I had not a minute to dry my hair or redo my face, so I let both go. For the first time I could remember, I cared not a whit about either. I exchanged my pants outfit for a dressy yellow blouse and long black satin skirt and then ran through the lobby to grab a taxi. Another jog through the lobby at my destination, and I arrived in the Sahara's main ballroom, which was filled with dinner tables for the show.

I found the three already seated and enjoying their meal. Not one of them asked about my damp, tangled hair or mascara-streaked cheeks . . . or why I cried throughout the dinner show. The stars were Sonny and Cher—a well-known singing/comedy duo—but nothing from the stage grabbed my attention. I sobbed into my linen napkin. It was dark in the ballroom, so thankfully, I was hidden from stares. I didn't know where the tears were coming from and was concerned about the flood of emotion. No one at the table questioned me. Odd, yes. But I was finding that God works in mysterious ways.

I called Pat the next day, and he assured me my tears were tears of joy and cleansing. He wasn't surprised at all!

"Just let the tears spill out. No need to be worried. This is common when someone is touched deeply by the Lord. It's the joy of the Lord. You've been rescued—from yourself. That was your fervent cry to God a few nights ago in your home, right? You're finding the joy to be uncontainable. This is a new emotion for you. You can't even find the words to explain it, can you?"

The words he spoke rang true. Yes, I was overflowing with joy—so happy to be found by God, to be cleansed by God, to taste an inexplicable freedom. Whenever I thought of the Lord, I'd start to cry. It was my way of offering Him thanks. My eyes were watery much of that week in Las Vegas, but my smile was wide and constant.

Pat and I met several more times during the remainder of my vacation with Bernie. Whether on the phone or in his dressing room, Pat obviously delighted in answering my continuing truckload of questions, and he used the Bible to do it.

One night before a performance, we were looking through some verses, and Pat almost missed his cue to be onstage. I could hear the orchestra playing the opening bars of his song. I yelled, "Pat, they're starting your first number!" "Oops! I'll run you through the roof of the ballroom. You can sit with the lighting men during the show." We ran above the ceiling to the spotlight room—me in my very high heels and Pat in his white buck shoes. He put me in the care of the crew and made it onstage at just the right moment, belting out, "Everything is beautiful in its own way . . ."

While I was up in the dark stage crew loft, the light of two great spiritual truths flooded my mind. First, I now accepted the reality that this personal God, to whom I had just committed myself, was powerfully active in my life. The circumstances of the recent days were much too precisely, perfectly, beautifully, elaborately arranged to be coincidences. *How big is God!*

Second, *I* was a changed person! Cigarettes were freely available in the casinos. I would reach for one, and then would decide to wait until later. I found myself ordering hot tea or orange juice instead of strong cocktails that made me lightheaded. I'd wander into the casino to gamble, then change my mind and meander off. My cursing ceased. I lost the desire to tell off-color jokes or to hear them. I lost all desire to watch any TV shows in our room. And I noticed a change in my morality when we were going through a hotel lobby to get to a restaurant. A nude show was in progress, and a glass wall to my left would have given me a good view of the entertainment. I turned my head in the opposite direction.

These choices were no longer a matter of willpower. I was not initiating this transformation. It just didn't seem to be what I wanted to do anymore. My heart was now turned towards a wondrous and *big* God, to whom I had never before given the slightest bit of attention. My value system had fundamentally changed. My thoughts were radically transformed. To say I was puzzled about this "new Judy" would be an understatement.

Baffled, I asked my mentor how it was possible for some of my poor habit patterns to change without my willfully choosing to do so. Pat showed me biblically how God's Holy

Spirit, now resident in me, was where the transformation was coming from. First I saw the changes showing up in my thoughts, my words, and my actions. Then, I as I began reading the Bible for the first time, I saw stories in the Old and New Testaments mirroring what I had experienced: the life-altering effects of turning Godward. I even experienced a healing in the physical realm. I noticed that the mild eczema I'd battled for years had totally disappeared! *How big is God!*

What a vacation! Unimaginable days. God had won me in Las Vegas! Leaving Pat Boone for home was, without exaggeration, the most difficult parting I'd ever experienced. It was more than just a matter of admiration and gratitude for what Pat had given me in time, kindness, and Bible instruction. My concern was that I knew no one outside of "Sin City" who loved God the way he did. I had come to understand that few individuals—whether observant Jewish people or church-going Gentiles—had any intimate experience with the powerful reality of a personal, interactive God. Pat was the only link to my "faith walk." I actually tried to convince Bernie to open a law practice in Beverly Hills. But Pat assured me God would go with me back to my home. He knew of a Baltimore couple who followed after God wholeheartedly, so he gave me their phone number.

On the flight home, I began to process all that had taken place and knew my life would never be the same. I had been a *wondering* Jew for many years, and now the deepest wonderings of my heart had found a home—in God alone. And then, somewhere over the vast prairies of Middle America, Bernie turned to me, smiling, and said, "Judy, you are a changed girl." I grinned. Until that moment, I wasn't aware others could see a difference in me.

All my efforts for all those years—self-imposed morality, expertise in various venues, philanthropic work, financial and social status, and finally, years of engaging in the falsehoods of cults—were motivated by a desire to hear precisely those words from someone who knew me well. Ten days earlier, I had raised my head to an unknown God and cried, "I'm trying to be a good person, and I don't know how to do it. Would you show me, if you exist, that you are able to change me?"

Bernie confirmed what I now knew. There's a Creator who is able to—and loves to—*change people*. This Creator God provided a Savior to make a way when there was no way. All the hoops I had jumped through never delivered on their promises. I thought, *Everyone needs a Savior. The Messiah (Savior) is, was, and ever shall be the Israelite Jesus.* This thought settled me spiritually, emotionally, and intellectually. *Any doubts, Judy? Any more wonderings?* Not one. How could I argue with my own powerful story, or with the prophesies in the Hebrew Scriptures? The thought came, *I can't possibly understand the depth of God's love because I can't fit this glorious God inside my little head. I'm going to need a bigger head.*

After deplaning—as a changed girl—in Baltimore, I stood off to the side while Bernie went to retrieve our luggage. Tears fell from my eyes again with the glorious, too-good-to-be-true thought, *God's grace is amazing. What a homecoming!* Well, not exactly as I thought it would be . . .

PART TWO
THE LIFE OF WONDER

*"You will never cease to be the most amazed person
on earth at what God has done for you on the inside."*
(Oswald Chambers, *My Utmost for His Highest*)

CHAPTER 17

TIES THAT BIND—LOOSED

When we arrived home, my "spiritual" groups embraced me with their arms, but not with their hearts. I came to them with the childlike joy of a six-year-old who had finally learned to ride a bike. Though no longer dependent on training wheels, I was still dependent—but on *the Trainer*. And it turned out to be a great exchange.

My fellow sojourners appeared happy for me but were eager to get back to spiritualism, New Age, and our various other "inherent goodness of man" philosophies. New Age thinking has no moral principles that are absolutely true and right for everyone; you create your own reality and your own truth. It's difficult to blame secular humanists for buying into such a man-centered gospel, because the idea sounds so good—namely, that we're not accountable to anyone higher than ourselves, so we never have to repent to God.

Having returned to Baltimore with only a smidgeon of Bible knowledge, I didn't realize that all I had been "living, eating, breathing" for a few years was abominable to God, according to Scripture. While with Pat Boone, I never thought to broach the subject of my spiritualist involvements. We were solely focused on exploring the foundations of my Jewish faith and the fulfillment of Messianic promises. Time didn't allow any delving into my current activities back at home.

Therefore, I continued with my groups, ignorant of their toxicity. The teachings always reinforced the idea that our life experiences were what really mattered. It was increasingly hard for me to understand how these Gentiles—to whom the stories of Jesus as Messiah was inoffensive—were more interested in things like spirits appearing at séances than they were in using the Bible for instruction. How deep my sadness was! My "spiritual" partners were more in tune with mystical and occult practices than with the "genuine article"; they were intent only on pursuing deeper or higher *subjective* religious experiences.

The groups were enslaved to what appeared good. But what they were caught up in was evil and corrupt—demonic, in fact, though none of our leaders ever used such a term. We attributed our guidance to angels or good spirits from the past, but the "help" we were getting from the "other world" had terrible ramifications. I was privy to some pretty sad and bizarre reports from individuals. By dabbling in the cults, we unknowingly were playing with fire.

I urged these close friends to measure everything we were doing by the best-selling volume of all time—one that had the signature of God on every page. I earnestly voiced to my cohorts that a Person was revealed within its cover, a "Soul Rescuer," who had great plans for those who sought him and him alone. I talked to them about mind control, self-realization studies, and the ideology of Humanism, which places man at the center of the equation as the source of all wisdom. In that way, man becomes a god unto himself. My comments resulted in nods from the listeners but no change in their plans or studies.

And then on a frigid morning in late January, three months after Las Vegas, Bernie called from his law office.

"How about flying to Montego Bay, Jamaica—tomorrow?"

"*Tomorrow?* Bernie, you're kidding. We have four children. How can we go?"

Our housekeeper, Essie, overheard the conversation, and quickly offered to babysit. For the rest of the day I prayed for a snowstorm. "All flights canceled" were the words I wanted to hear. The reason? I knew Jamaica, like Vegas, was just another tourist trap. Anyway, I doubted it could be God's will to send us there so soon after the Nevada vacation.

Reluctantly, I packed for the trip that evening. At one point I took a break and flipped open a magazine sent by a friend of Pat Boone's. There before me was a photo of a building, with a caption that read, "Chatham Hotel, Montego Bay, Jamaica, home of the Holy Spirit Teaching Mission." My heart gave a response. I considered, *Could this be another providential "Las Vegas experience"?*

The next day we flew to a banana haven—the lush green island of Jamaica. I carried the latest Edgar Cayce book as my reading material. Since Cayce had at times referred to Jesus in his teachings, I didn't know how to sort out the differences between my two spiritual worlds.

Easy-going Bernie helped me get in touch with the Chatham Hotel, the home of the mission, and we were invited to stop in. The two of us—Bernie, a bit hesitant and I, a bit excited—were welcomed by a handsome, smiling British couple, Trevor and Sue Lancashire.

"Please, tell us about yourselves" I asked after we settled on soft cushioned wicker chairs and were served proper British tea and scones. Trevor told how God had miraculously healed his back when they lived in Britain. Doctors hadn't been able to give him any relief from a badly deteriorated disk that left him completely incapacitated. By that time, he had no hope for the future.

Trevor recounted that one day, a former coworker came to their home and asked to pray for him: "God raised me up completely whole. When I walked down the stairs, Sue looked up at me in shock—this couldn't be her husband who had been so racked with pain and bedridden!" Soon after, the Lord set Trevor free of an addiction to various cults, thereby adding spiritual healing to the physical. Bernie and I were awestruck! As the visit ended, the gracious Brits invited us to dinner the next evening. My husband's response: "Thank you. Yes!"

Before we drove there the next day, I had time alone in our ocean-side room while Bernie walked on the beach. I spent the time entreating God, wanting to know whether accepting Jesus as Messiah was a more advanced path on the road I had been traveling all along. Again, had I taken a small chunk of time to fill Pat in on my "extracurricular" activities, he could have exposed the deceitful philosophies once and for all. Since that never occurred, I still needed to know.

And so my ardent petition began with: "Do you want me to continue with my groups? Are Cayce's teachings, as well as my other spiritual practices—which I still find powerfully captivating—okay? Do you want me to use my past years' knowledge and experiences? Would you like me to teach reincarnation to fellow followers of yours, Lord? One more thing: Just *in case* my thinking is faulty, would you please make it *really* clear?"

Shortly thereafter, Bernie and I headed over to the Lancashire home. The visits with these dear Brits in their simple abode was a bit different than visiting with all-American Pat Boone in a lavish hotel, but as I was soon to discover, it was nevertheless another remarkable "set-up" by God.

About 7 p.m. we arrived at their place. Sue announced, "I'm serving you a 'jerk' meal." I mistakenly thought she said, "I'm serving you jerks a meal." Laughter pealed when Sue explained she was using a spice called "jerk"! Before we took the first bite of the native Jamaican jerk-seasoned dinner, I kicked Bernie under the table. He was a picky eater, so the wifely nudge signaled him to swallow the food with not one grimace.

We two couples were quite compatible, though Bernie chose to sit on the sidelines when our hosts and I decided to pray and praise God for his goodness. As we began, all of a sudden Trevor declared, "The Lord says, 'I am the only perfect one. I am the only true wisdom. Trust in me, rest in me, and I will show you miracles like you've never seen before. I will show you healings and impossible things that you've never seen before. Forget all that natural man has taught you, and I will show you.'"

Following those words, Trevor described something he was seeing, as in a vision. "An axe has come to the root of a huge tree. The tree itself is ostensibly dead and severed from its base. There's a giant tree stump left, upon which a few residual twigs continue to kick with life. There's new healthy growth waiting to shoot up from the stump, but some old living limbs are hindering."

Trevor and Sue agreed that none of the words—or the vision—fit them. Suddenly, I knew the Lord was speaking about me! No one in the room but Bernie knew of my involvement in the world of cults and New Age.

There was a lengthy silence. My thoughts ran this way: *The Lord had certainly brought the axe to "the old tree" when I accepted Jesus as the Messiah. I've been separated from the power of the invisible enemy, Satan, and from demonic spirits. These deceptive influences have worked throughout my entire life to keep me from the knowledge of*

God's truth. Though a changed person, I'm still holding on to other belief systems, trying to join the new to the old. God must be indicating through Trevor that in order for my life to be fruitful, every twig on the tree stump must die. All leftovers of my former dependence on New Age, parapsychology, and its corollaries must go.

I thought about Trevor's words, *"I will show you miracles like you've never seen before. I will show you healings and impossible things that you've never seen before. Forget all that natural man has taught you and I will show you."* I had already been part of and witnessed sensational occurrences within the enclave of parapsychology. But the signs and wonders experienced by me and my fellow seekers were seductive and ruinous. The "goings-on" led us down paths that first appeared spectacular and good, but later displayed spiritual filth. So when God spoke through Trevor, "Forget what you've learned from natural man," I knew the Lord was referring to false prophets and teachers who had polluted my life in recent years.

Though not realizing that Trevor had just exercised one of the spiritual gifts listed in the Bible—the gift of knowledge—I knew in my heart it was fashioned for me. It was an admonishment from God, who saw what my godly dinner host did not know about me. How could Trevor have known unless the Holy Spirit revealed it to him?

I recalled the night in my den when, while crying out to God in emptiness and helplessness, I named the name of Jesus. Yes, my actions were biblical, but I didn't realize this since I knew no Scripture. What I *did* know was that Someone had touched me, and transformed me. My dilemma that night in Baltimore was, I possessed no logical tools to explain what was beyond description.

Tonight was similar. I was right in the middle of another powerful touch from heaven. My understanding was less than dim as to why my practices, all these years, were toxic. But, one thing *was* clear. *I had just received God's response to my hotel room plea.* I broke the silence with: "Trevor, what you just said is for me. Without your personal knowledge, I was dialoging with God late today about this other world I live in. I realize that though I'm now a worshiper of the living God, there are still idols in my life—idols that imitate truth."

Following my response, in obedience to God, I audibly renounced "my other world." There were several pauses on my part in order to collect my thoughts and ensure all was brought to the table. By the time I finished, those in the room, and more importantly the Lord, heard me relinquish—out loud!— my involvement with Edgar Cayce, the Ouija board, séances, divination, clairvoyance, mental telepathy, aurascopes, Rosicrucianism, all occult philosophies, Eastern religions, reincarnation, delving into past lives, psychics, astrology, card-reading, palm-reading, self-hypnosis, automatic writing, New Age philosophy, self-help disciplines—to name just a few! It was quite a recitation since I did not want to leave one stone unturned or to have one unholy twig still kicking with life. On returning to my hotel room, I eagerly tore up the Edgar Cayce book I was reading. I felt clean, free, and at peace with God. This wondrous God had led me once again to a place far from home for his purposes—the Lord's power and love were overwhelming me.

CHAPTER 18

UP IN FLAMES!

When we returned from Montego Bay, my group again welcomed me with open arms. But as I spoke of the trip, the faces of these stunned listeners clearly reflected closed minds and hardened hearts. With conviction, I boldly tackled the subject of New Age philosophy: "Do you realize that self-consciousness and self-centeredness shape the operating system of New Age, rather than surrender to God's powerful love and purposes? We are not glorifying the Lord one iota. Instead, by turning to what we call our 'inner selves,' *we* are being glorified."

I continued, hoping not to be long-winded, but wanting every word to count toward dismantling the horrific worldview we had trusted. My heart was in my throat, as I knew I was treading on my audience's sacred ground.

"New Age techniques cause us to work hard in order to become *nicer, better.* We're led to depend on 'me, myself, and I' for the transformation. Everything to which we give time and energy actually turns us *inward* rather than Godward;

therefore we have been deceived. Can you grasp what I just said? *Deceived!*"

Pushing through any remaining trepidation, I spoke to the sham of our "mystical" searchings—astrology, séances, Cayce, and reincarnation. I hurled them out, along with all the other studies and activities that were leading our souls astray. For emphasis, I repeated, "The 'religion' we've been practicing is detrimental to our souls."

I was met with tight-lipped stares. Sad and spent, I drove home. My only solace: I would sleep in peace, for the pronouncements were spoken with genuine love and compelling concern. I couldn't yet communicate using the Bible, since I knew so little of it, but what I shared came from a heart that had received quite a liberating mercy in Jamaica. (And the freeing words had resonated incredibly clear and authentic with a crisp British accent!)

The evening had been pivotal. I knew that remaining under the influence of my old belief systems would break my growing closeness with God. In fact, it would be nothing less than rebellious. So the passing days found me fully invested in reflecting upon the Scriptures—I was daily giving to the Lord time and energy that formerly had been wasted on pursuing other gods. I canceled everything that might prevent my knowing God better, including the weekly home gatherings centered on Edgar Cayce.

Several weeks later, I received a call from Dr. Lawton Smith, a leading Florida eye surgeon and an acquaintance of Pat Boone. "Judy, would you come to Orlando and share what happened in your life recently?" (This would be the first time I told my story before a large audience.) Lawton then spoke about a friend who was immersed in the Edgar Cayce cult. "Could you make time for lunch with Jean? She needs to hear what God has shown you."

I agreed to come, although I was nervous about a lunch with this Jean. On the plane, I opened my Bible and did some research, including sections I was reading for the first time. To my amazement, I found very specific passages describing God's perspective on much of what I'd held dear for years. I was totally absorbed by the discoveries I was making—what remarkable treasures were hidden in those leather-bound pages. Now, *finally,* I was gaining the intellectual understanding I needed.

> "Let no one be found among you who sacrifices their son or daughter in the fire, who practices divination or sorcery, interprets omens, engages in witchcraft, or casts spells, or who is a medium or spiritist or who consults the dead. Anyone who does these things is detestable to the LORD; because of these same detestable practices the LORD your God will drive out those nations before you." (Deuteronomy 18:10-12).

Discovering this passage proved to be a spiritual marker in my life. What I'd only caught a glimpse of in Jamaica, I now clearly saw in *Scripture.* I met Jean at a quiet eatery near my hotel and opened to Deuteronomy while we sat together. Ignoring our egg salad sandwiches, the two of us read on, eyes widening as we found other verses verifying that enchanters, sorcerers, and astrologers were outside of God's will. They were practicing arts forbidden to his children. I hadn't known till this moment that even *astrology* was condemned in the Bible. What a revelation to me!

I was thrilled when Jean came to freedom and was delivered from New Age and Cayce right at the table. She wanted her life to have purpose; she wanted righteousness within. Jean was a reflection of who I was just a few months back. The good news had found a place in her too!

Now that I had gleaned *from the Bible* what God's judgment was on spiritualism—"Abomination!"—I came home from Orlando and discarded all my parapsychology books, self-help New Age materials, the Ouija board, and other occult paraphernalia. Into a fire they went! That's what the Lord commanded the Israelites to do with such things. Pagan nations engaged in those evil practices, and the Israelites were not to follow their lead. And so ended my years of ignorance, when I was enthusiastically, though naively, serving Satan.

Yet, as I stared into the fire, I was actually counting *as priceless* my years serving those false gods. Why? So that the abomination may be exposed. "It takes one to know one," the saying goes. From then on, if I found myself around someone espousing fallacies, my sensitive antennae would go up. I recognized the language, knew the ramifications, was ready, willing, able, and—more importantly—equipped. I had tasted the false; I now tasted the true. What word would I use to describe the taste of truth? For me, truth *satisfied;* I was comfortably full, not wanting anything else. My hunger for self-help directives and "bowing down" to false gods was astonishingly, finally squelched.

CHAPTER 19

REJECTIONS OF THE HIGHEST CALIBER

I had tasted rejection from my "searcher" friends, but now I sensed a greater rejection ahead, as I contemplated *how* to tell, *when* to tell, or *whether* to tell family. Then there was also my wonderful, successful, intelligent circle of Jewish friends. *Help, Lord! May I just live in my pantry with popcorn and lemonade until the world ceases to exist?*

My mother called exactly one day after I cut ties with my "other-world-people" (Mom's name for them). "You know, Judy dear, we've talked so much about my grandchildren that I've not yet heard about your Las Vegas vacation. Which stars did you see? Did you win enough for Daddy and me to buy a condo in West Palm Beach?"

We laughed, but now the ball was in my court. I chose to spill out the whole story, despite hearing somewhere in the recesses of my mind, *Oy vey—no way, Judy! What are you doing?* I spoke at a rapid pace, not wanting Mom to have a chance to interject *anything*! When finished, I held my breath. Except for a few disapproving "Hmms," the silence on the other end spoke volumes. Then came slow, carefully chosen words and behind them, I could hear anger rising: "Well, honey, it sounds as though you've been brainwashed, or maybe even hypnotized."

There was nothing more to do but hang up since both of us were a bit upset—I, from telling all; Mom, from hearing all. A simple "Goodbye, Judy," "Bye, Mom" ended the conversation. Shortly thereafter, when Mom came from Philadelphia to visit, she was dismayed to discover her daughter was reading the New Testament. (I had left it on an end table.) *Oy!*

On hearing of my transformation, other family members, were equally disturbed. Screaming and red in the face, my stepfather came out with: "You're just going through a phase! If you still believe this ten years from now, I'll listen to you!" He cursed the name of Jesus to me and joined my mother in angry proclamations.

My in-laws adjusted in their own way. Bernie's dad pretended nothing was different. His mom? She wept quietly when no one was around and paced around the apartment at night, depressed.

Someone told me my adored grandmother, mother, mother-in-law, and aunt met to find a way to have me committed to a mental institution for treatment or deprogramming. But worst of all, my brilliant, wealthy birth father chose to disown me. Though he was a bit distant, I held him close to my heart, so this was deeply hurtful. My stepmother spit on the floor (in a hospital no less!) when Bernie's aunt told her what had occurred.

One afternoon, my favorite college sorority sisters gathered at a luncheon to hear me tell my story. Not one of them asked a single question, nor was there any show of interest, though their graciousness to "hear me out" meant so much. Down the road, a few of my hometown Philadelphia high school friends severed our relationship.

What about Bernie? He would joke with me, "I'll accept Jesus as the Promised One when I come back in another lifetime as a non-Jew." But he had seen me change as a wife and mother, and there was no denying that his spouse wasn't the same person. I knew privately it was something Bernie couldn't write off.

While considered a traitor who had betrayed the Jewish religion, I deeply understood the reactions from family and friends. Most Jewish people are raised with the strong message that we must stick together. This fierce loyalty has come out of our long history of persecution and rejection. Oh, how I wanted all of them to see my Jewishness was now both biblical and *complete*. It was no longer just cultural, no longer just about our wonderful "to die for" foods, no longer just about Israel and Zionism, and no longer just about social issues and Jewish charity work. Now I really loved and worshiped God in a close and personal way and I also loved the Bible.

Ironically, the problem for all my Jewish connections was the Israelite, Jesus. I knew the truth about him *intellectually* through the Bible and *experientially* through my story. What could I do but be faithful to him because of such truth? I was still "Judy" in personality, in temperament, and in appearance. But my heart was made new with peace, joy, and the knowledge of a wonderful waiting eternity, which was infinitely more important than my few short years on earth.

Soon after we returned from Las Vegas, I began to hunt for a rabbi who taught from the Old Testament prophecies. I had asked Pat Boone, "What's a prophecy?" And he answered, "It's when God describes a future event—long before it happens—through a servant, known as a prophet.

The odds of someone fulfilling a few hundred prophecies are too great to even number. It's impossible."

I asked, "How many prophecies in the Old Testament did Jesus fulfill?"

"All of them! Judy, Jesus perfectly fulfilled every last prophecy that pointed to the coming Messiah, to his life and death."

I thought perchance I had missed all the prophetic teachings because my attendance at Shabbat services had been scarce. But now, I began to attend Shabbat services at a different shul (synagogue) every Friday night to see if they did, in fact, talk about a coming Messiah. Week after week the sermons centered on Zionism, family, community, serving one another, fundraising, and the suffering of Soviet Jews. Yes, the sermons would spring from a portion of the Bible. However the application would be humanistic, not inspiring me to draw near to God or teaching me the "hows" of loving him with all my heart, soul, and strength.

Where was a teaching on heaven or sheol (hell), as mentioned in Scripture? Most importantly, where were sermons about prophecies relating to my need for a Messiah? How would I recognize him? What would happen when he came? Where would he be born? How would he die? My Bible reading was revealing the answers in the Old Testament. Sitting in synagogue, I'd think, *Dear Rabbi, these are life-and-death issues. Why are you not bringing these subjects to us in your messages?* I tried—really tried—to integrate what had happened to me just weeks before with any one of the sermons I was hearing.

After Shabbat, I'd go home and immerse myself in the Bible. Providentially, the Holy Spirit was drawing me to the Gospels—those real-life stories of Jesus. I read eagerly, intrigued by the way Jesus lived out the love of his Father during his brief thirty-three years here on earth.

The profound maxims of the Teacher challenged me, but there was something more. Jesus' strong leadership and compassionate ministry comforted the deepest parts of my soul. I was learning and applying God's principles because I wanted to do so, not because I had to. I found yielding to Him gave my life purpose and deep inner fulfillment. It was staggering to know that I am personally and unconditionally loved by God. *Imagine!*

I signed up for "religion" classes at synagogue. My intention: *Teach me, Rabbi. Please answer my questions!* On the first day the rabbi opened the class up for discussion. He wanted us to participate, so I raised my hand. I asked him about Saul of Tarsus, a Hebrew scholar, Pharisee and zealot, who on the road to Damascus had a supernatural heavenly visitation. It had happened as he'd been traveling to arrest fellow Jews who were convinced Jesus was the promised Messiah. Saul was enraged by such "heresy," his purpose was to have them violently killed for their beliefs.

This respected zealot got my attention, since his supernatural experience was similar to mine on that cold January day in Baltimore when I was lifted into another realm. The first time I read about Saul of Tarsus, my reaction was, *What! This happened to him also? Over 2,000 years ago, another Jewish person was blinded by the same glorious light? He heard the same awesome, thunderous voice I had?* The words from heaven to Saul (and me) pointed to Jesus and radically changed us both. At the same time he heard the words, the power of God fell upon Saul, causing him to fall from his horse to the ground. Had I been on a horse instead of my bed, I would have hit the ground too!

After relating the story of Saul to the rabbi (but without mentioning anything about my similar story), I added, "Rabbi, Saul's teacher was the renowned Rabbi Gamaliel, a leading teacher of the Law of Moses, whom I've heard you quote in services. What was it that happened on the road to Damascus to his brilliant student? How would you explain it?" The rabbi's answer to me, in front of the others, was that Saul had had an epileptic fit, which explained the fall off the horse.

"Where is that found in any historical account, Rabbi?" I then tentatively asked, "Were *all* the Jewish disciples— thousands of them who followed Jesus as Messiah—were they all epileptics?"

Continuing, I mentioned to the rabbi that those who rejected Jesus were the legalistic, self-righteous religious authorities, not the common Israelites who were needy, humble, and mistreated by those leaders. I sensed uneasiness in the rabbi, who through his studies, would have been acquainted with Rabbi Gamaliel's shining prodigy, Saul. He knew, for sure, that Saul, who was later renamed Paul, went on to write much of the New Testament.

"You ask interesting questions, Judy." That was the extent of his response as he turned to the rest of the class and asked, "Are there any other questions?"

"Wait, I'd like to ask one more, Rabbi. As a child, I loved the stories I learned in Sunday school with all the amazing Hebrew characters. I recently read the Gospels in the New Testament and was enthralled by the luminous historical figure of the Jesus the Nazarene. I read how he came to complete the law and the prophets. I'm finding that Christianity is incomprehensible without Judaism, just as Judaism is not complete without Christianity. Could it be that the New Testament is a supplement to the Jewish scriptures and not a separate historical manuscript, meant only for the non-Jew?"

I had brought a Bible with me (the only person who did). "May I read something from a historical manuscript, Rabbi?"

"Go ahead, Judy."

"When Gamaliel was asked if it was possible that Jesus could be the long-awaited Messiah, here is what he answered: 'If it be of men, it will come to naught, but if it be of God, ye will not be able to overthrow it; lest perhaps ye be found even to fight against God.'"

I continued, "Rabbi, the belief of great multitudes throughout the ages has shown that what Jesus said and did—including being raised from the dead and having been seen by hundreds—has not come to naught. The acceptance by untold millions that Jesus was the long awaited Messiah never came to 'naught.'"

I respectfully asked him, "I wonder what Rabbi Gamaliel, Saul's teacher, would say now if he were with us?" My questions were ignored. The subject was changed. Needless to say, I lost favor with the rabbi.

The time came when I no longer attended classes or Friday night services. The rabbi's sermons, in past years, had never touched below the surface of my soul to effect change. None of his messages gave me encouragement of any kind to read the Bible *for myself,* nor did they offer any help on how to develop a personal prayer life. "Shooting words up" to God when in need was not enough. I wanted a genuine time of devotion in order to bring my flaws to God, to praise, to ask, and to worship him. I had had no model for that—ever.

The believers I was meeting were a diverse group, but all shared a common denominator: "Once I was lost; now I am found. Once I was blind; now I can see."

Soon enough, I discovered the majority of Gentiles were pretty much like the old me. Lip service was prevalent and church attendance was saved for holidays and weddings.

The first year following Las Vegas was really a wonder year: To my delight and more so God's, my "cute as a button" Jewish sister-in-law became my first family member to discover the Messiah. After hearing my story and others', she wanted what she was hearing about and seeing with her own eyes—a strong relationship with God. This was the first person I led in prayer to accept God's amazing salvation. Our family now had two who had been persuaded to put the Lord first. We were a great support for one another. If only we could have bottled our trust in God. It was so real we wanted to offer it on the streets!

CHAPTER 20

A WANDERING JEW AND A HUSBAND MADE NEW

The "*wondering* Jew" years had ended and the "*wandering* Jew" years began. Invitations to tell my story came pouring in from all over. What precipitated the calls? Was it my Jewish background? Or was it celebrity Pat Boone's involvement? Or was it my deliverance from the snare of cults? Yes, yes, and yes. *All three* led to interest nationwide—and across the border into Canada. Bernie's response to the requests: "Honey, if you can help people, if you can bless others, please go and do it." While he wasn't interested in God for himself, my husband was gracious and accommodating.

The children were gracious in sending me out, too, but it wasn't for the same reason. You see, I'd create all kinds of healthy meals before a speaking engagement, and when I left the house, the freezer bulged. Oddly, I'd return home to find the freezer still bulging. I came to find out the head of the household was taking his happy children to places like McDonald's for dinner and Dunkin Donuts for dessert. This father/chauffeur was happy as well, since he preferred hamburgers and donuts to my broccoli or spinach casseroles. Saying he ate plenty of spinach when he young, Bernie would kid me: "I wanted to grow up strong enough to refuse it!"

To his credit, Bernie would make sure the children ate something nutritious while I was gone—maybe half an apple. I'd query them all when I returned. "Did everyone have some fruit while I was away?"

"Certainly, dear."

"Yes, Mommy."

Just as Bernie took charge of meals during my absence, our housekeeper Essie kept everything clean and tidy. She prayed for me daily, just as she'd done long before Pat Boone came on the scene. Las Vegas had brought me home with twinkling eyes and plenty of smiles. Like Bernie, she recognized that I was a new woman. So all the bases were covered while I was away, maybe not perfectly, but my home was full of happy campers—especially happy eaters.

As the months passed, calls to speak for events, radio programs, and television shows kept me as busy as I wanted to be. At first, I just told my story. But all that changed when a group in Wilmington, Delaware requested my return. This invitation pressed me to develop my first biblical teaching. At first I was given hour-long segments at banquets and the like, but then I was asked to do full weekend retreats and conferences. At some events, I was speaking to thousands of people.

Interestingly, of the two of us, Bernie was the people person. I preferred seclusion. Reading continued to be my favorite activity, albeit the majority of my reading was now chosen for its "faith fuel." Others' stories were tremendously inspiring! This quote by Desiderius Erasmus is an apt description of me in those days: "When I get a little money, I buy books; and if any is left, I buy food and clothes."

I grabbed solitude whenever I could get it. My humorous and gregarious public persona belied my truly introverted heart. I was most content on a sofa, curled up with steaming hot cocoa (garnished with mini-marshmallows, of course), watching winter's white flakes coat all of nature. In fact, it shouldn't be hard to find me in heaven, since I'll be living on the snowy side. Most everyone else will long for the beach side—so they tell me. But how big is God to catapult someone into the spotlight who prefers privacy, books, and being snowed under . . . without a shovel.

My preparation for a one-hour teaching required about eighteen hours of Bible study and listening for God to impress my heart. When doing retreats and conferences, I might be speaking for five sessions. The groundwork I put in to prepare was a huge and glorious investment of my time. Diligent study habits from my school days came back into play. Spontaneous speaking? If I had to, yes, I would—and sometimes did, but *I no liked!*

Also, it was very important to me that every teaching had to be born out of a personal understanding, a real-life experience. I had to "own" the Bible passages I was expounding. Therefore, every seminar was based on my being a "guinea pig" for God. It appeared he had to try everything out on me *first* before the truths were passed forward. *Oy vey!* But you know, that's how I learned God's principles, tasted his mercy, and understood the consequences of wrongdoing. I could teach only that which I accepted for myself. Then, and only then, did I feel comfortable passing it forward.

What about Bernie, who gave me space and encouragement to study and communicate well? Spiritually, the one person I most longed to walk hand-in-hand with was my husband.

Our home had become an open door to visiting missionaries from around the world and others whose joy was in the Lord. Bernie welcomed everyone. In addition, he took great pleasure in meeting the needs of people who had little of the world's goods. I'd see him giving his possessions away—a good sweater, a valued watch. One time, he even removed his coat and handed it to someone who didn't have one. He was generous with money also. Yet, he was not a worshiper of God. Raised more strictly devout than I had been, he in some ways had farther to travel. But God was patiently drawing Bernie to himself.

About four years after I'd acknowledged that Jesus was the Messiah, Bernie flew with me to California, where I would attend a convention. He made himself clear before we left: "I'm going to sit by the pool, and you can go to all the meetings you want." His statement brought to mind my very own before going to Las Vegas: "Bernie, I'm staying in the hotel room. You can go to all the shows you want." God had other ideas for Bernie, as he had had for me. Jehovah's providence was soon to be seen once again . . .

The day after we arrived, Bernie skipped sitting in a lounge chair by the pool, deciding instead to join me for the day's opening session. We sat holding hands among 15,000 attendees who were thrilled to be attending this international conference. The singing, the sermons, and the fellowship allowed Bernie to sense God's presence. Heaven came down on this Jewish man! Bernard "no middle name" Reamer was powerfully wooed by the Lord. I felt him release my hand, leaving his seat in the uppermost balcony to make his way far down to the arena floor. He, along with a few hundred others, went to humbly ask for prayer.

My tears were falling in thanksgiving and surprise. I could barely spot him, but I knew he was fine—finer than he'd ever been in his life. In terms of physical distance from my seat to where he stood, Bernie may have been far away, but spiritually, from that moment on, the gap was closed. We left Anaheim, California, as prayer partners. *How big is God! My joy was overflowing!*

Who would have thought this could be possible? But God has ways and means—he knew how to draw even the gentle Jewish boy I met at the University of Maryland, who had told me weeks before leaving for this California trip, "I'm just going to sit by the pool while you go to meetings." And the angels were smiling and winking at each other when Bernie the attorney made that declaration.

This "new" husband made significant changes to his law practice, offering clients counsel based on biblical principles and prayer for those who were willing. He continued to be detailed and highly organized in his legal work. In addition, Bernie had a quiet demeanor, was a superb listener, and always returned clients' calls in a timely manner. That combination made him a popular lawyer—and in fact, he had the largest practice of all independent attorneys in Baltimore. My mother had much to brag about—grandchildren *and* her son-in-law. But, her enthusiasm to brag on Bernie was going to take a crazy turn . . .

CHAPTER 21

A GOVERNMENT POSITION IMPOSSIBLE TO REFUSE

A short two years after Bernie yielded to God's redemptive love on the West Coast, a trial of monumental magnitude on the East Coast stopped Bernie in his tracks. Though it presented a huge challenge to him in many ways, what occurred was a profound proving of Bernie's faith in God.

After initiating a sweeping investigation of physicians in several large cities, including Baltimore, the federal government indicted a number of doctors. Prosecutors exposed these physicians for padding patients' invoices before submitting them for insurance reimbursement. In situations of workmen's compensation cases or vehicular accidents, most patients had secured a lawyer, so the corrupted bills were mailed by the attorney's office.

After rounding up the dishonest doctors, federal authorities began indicting lawyers connected to these cases. Bernie ended up on the list, never imagining that he was passing along falsified doctor bills to insurance agencies.

In order to avoid a costly, tedious battle with the federal government, the other indicted lawyers pled guilty to just one count. Whether or not they were innocent, the penalty would be light—a minor black mark on their reputation. But for Bernie, this "reasonable" option wasn't an option. He would tell the truth and chance losing in a human court rather than be guilty of lying in God's court.

The young federal prosecutor argued with him. "Mr. Reamer, either you plead guilty on at least one count or you will go to prison, get stuck with a huge fine, and be disbarred. You went through all that schooling and built up a great clientele. You could lose it all unless you cooperate with me. C'mon, Mr. Reamer, would you really do that to your family?"

Bernie felt like punching him but instead answered calmly, "I have never collaborated with doctors in any criminal activities. I've always respected doctors and wouldn't have imagined they'd lie about patients' visits. I refuse to commit perjury in order to save myself, but instead will trust God with my life, my family, and my career. I plead 'not guilty.'"

Consequently, Bernie was indicted on twenty-four counts of mail fraud—one for each falsified bill submitted to an insurance company from his office. Instead of securing a competent lawyer to the tune of $100,000, we both felt the Lord instructing Bernie to enter court *without* an attorney, but *with* twelve legal-size pages of handwritten scriptures. These holy nuggets of "wisdom from above" would be life-sustaining during those long, media-covered days in court.

The government secured thirty-two witnesses, all but four of whom were, at the time, incarcerated. It was common knowledge that novice prosecutors would plea-bargain with inmates in order to win cases and gain clout. The incarcerated would gladly say whatever they were instructed in exchange for a reduced prison term.

We listened in disbelief to complete fabrications given by already convicted criminals. A sense of justice naturally rears up in self-defense. But Bernie believed he was to remain silent unless prompted by the Lord. He objected only one time—a prisoner accused Bernie of counseling him on a particular date to drive his car into a pole, so an accident claim would be larger. Bernie stood and simply said, "Your honor, on that day I was on vacation in Pennsylvania and have the receipts."

Adding to the court drama was testimony from three doctors who had already pleaded guilty to bill falsification. To the chagrin of the assistant district attorney, they all testified Mr. Reamer knew nothing of their inaccurate invoices. And they were government witnesses! Surely the jury would give weight to the doctors' vindication of Bernie and also discredit the inmates' fabricated testimonies. Bernie would be found innocent—we just knew it. After all, the Lord of all was on his side. God would be his advocate! *Your reputation is at stake here, Lord. Our friends and family are waiting to see if you are as wonderful, real, and powerful as we claim.*

Ah, but the jury found him guilty on all twenty-four counts! It was the government's final witness—the thirty-second one—who ultimately had the most influence on the jury. The person was someone who had read of Bernie's indictment in the paper and gone to the prosecutor. This witness appeared credible, yet was filled with murderous vengeance from a past incident that involved Bernie and others.

The lawyer had saved the "believable" witness for the end, convinced this particular testimony would override any prior "Mr. Reamer is innocent" conclusions tentatively reached by the jurors. On the stand, the government witness spoke convincingly. "I swear to the fact Mr. Reamer told me he was in league with doctors to defraud insurance companies."

It was a blatant lie, but Bernie couldn't prove he never said such a thing. What it came down to was one person's word against another's. Though blindsided by this unexpected outcome, my husband and I—now both strong in faith—were in full agreement. Our lives and this trial were ultimately covered and cared for by the Lord. God, we knew, wasn't shaken by this shocking turn of events. I was, though!

I went home after the trial, climbed into bed, and pulled the covers up over my face. I was numb with shock, having firmly believed God would reward Bernie's honesty. Wondering where we went wrong, I began to struggle with God. *I'm never getting off this bed, Lord. Life is so hard. Was our faith not strong enough? Did I not trust you fully to vindicate Bernie? Should he have hired a lawyer? But, we strongly sensed you were directing otherwise.*

Bernie could have pled guilty on one count of mail fraud and received just a slap on the wrist. Instead, he had claimed Proverbs 3:5-6 as a watchword from the start of the investigation: **"Trust in the Lord with all your heart; and lean not unto your own understanding. In all your ways acknowledge him, and he shall direct your paths."**

As I was lying on my bed expressing worry after worry to God, he began to overlay them with his wisdom. *Judy, lack of faith didn't cause the loss of the case. In fact, if there were report cards, you and Bernie would have earned A's in faith. But a "beyond-reason" plan is already in place that doesn't hinge on Bernie's innocence. There is something higher going on in the heavenlies. My plan for Bernie and you takes precedence over the court's decision. You are in my will. Judy, trust me.*

Once the Lord had illuminated his words in my spirit, I was at rest. I rose up from the ashes, revitalized with this key thought: *There is a good God-plan already in motion that doesn't depend on Bernie being found "not guilty."* This revelation became indelibly written upon my heart. What a comfort it was to me from that point on.

Bernie was ordered to pay many thousands of dollars in fines. He was also required to permanently forfeit his attorney's license, along with his right to vote. And finally, Bernie was to be imprisoned four years on each of the twenty-four counts—altogether a ninety-six-year prison term! Just as a guilty person can slip through the cracks and go free, so might an innocent person slip through the cracks unjustly and find himself behind bars.

Bernie's father, an attorney, ranted, "What! Are you crazy? Appeal the case!" Our Jewish friends echoed the sentiment. My father, the judge—I could only imagine his thoughts! Since he had disowned me, I was never to know them for sure. And the truth is, had I heard his "two cents," staying the course would have been much harder.

After much prayer, we knew not to appeal the case, but to accept the verdict. There was a godly rest in our souls—a priceless peace to possess. Before the sentencing actually took place (a couple of months later), the judge received letters from Pat Boone, Chuck Colson, and other influential people, attesting to Bernie's character. And I believe it's because of their efforts that the judge was merciful and Bernie's sentence was reduced—to four years! Ultimately, thanks are due to a great God, who impressed these respected people to appeal to the judge on Bernie's behalf.

The federal prison where Maryland offenders were always sent was in nearby Pennsylvania. To our shock, and everyone else's, Bernie was sent instead to a prison at Eglin Air Force Base, Fort Walton Beach, Florida—a thousand miles away. How could this be? No one had ever heard of this happening before. What an inconsiderate judge! How could the children and I visit Bernie? We'd never even heard of Fort Walton Beach and needed a map to locate it.

I flew with Bernie to Pensacola, Florida, drove an hour to Eglin, stopped at the prison gate, and kissed him good-bye. It was emotionally gut-wrenching. But spiritually, we were graced to stand strong. I then returned home to take care of our four young ones.

In this new journey of trusting God, we were becoming *better* rather than *bitter.* Had we not come to know and trust in God's "beyond belief" goodness, "bitter" would have been our ultimate fate. Instead, a friend spoke these words to our hurting emotions: "It's real; it's different; but it's not bad." She explained, "This *really* has happened; your life will *never* be the same; but it is *not bad,* because *God is good.*" I have since repeated that sentence to myself time and time again—and passed it forward time and time again.

During Bernie's incarceration, he was blessed with an office job assignment. And because of his efficient work ethic, Bernie was afforded multiple hours each day to immerse himself in the Bible. Before long, he connected with another prisoner with a similar passion. Together, they started the first Bible study on the premises, which is now a permanent part of the prison program. A wonder! Slowly but surely, God was beginning to clue us in to the wisdom of his ways.

Eventually, I rented out our home in Baltimore and leased a small house in Pensacola. Living in close proximity to the prison enabled the children and me to visit Bernie on weekends. My mother, embarrassed, told her friends in Philadelphia, "Judy, Bernie, and my four darling grandchildren moved to Florida because the government offered Bernie a position he just couldn't refuse." (How could I not laugh at how Mother covered up the real reason?)

Bernie never maneuvered to get out of prison early but depended on God to pick the date. And in God's merciful providence, Bernie's four-year sentence was reduced. He was released after serving only fourteen months! Once he fulfilled his six-month halfway-house requirement, God impressed upon Bernie and me to take up permanent residence near the emerald waters by the Gulf of Mexico—in Pensacola, a beautiful vacation spot. The Gulf is a recreation area, and we drove off to the beach frequently, building castles in the sugar-white sand with the children. How we needed this! I once again was taken with the wonders of a powerful God who had chosen to redeem even the worst of situations.

The move from the familiar East Coast gave us, for the first time, the freedom to exercise our spiritual faith. At times it had been a bit debilitating emotionally to sense the judgment of family and friends I once considered close. There was a strong temptation to stay in the same habit patterns and to keep performing as others expected us to behave. It sapped our energy and at times saddened our hearts. Moving to another location changed that, but when it came to prayer, this was no "out of sight, out of mind" situation: I prayed more—not less—for our relatives and friends. Sincere prayer can be uttered from the summit of Mt. Everest or behind bars, as well as from the Deep South.

I was learning that when God said "No" to our particular prayer requests ("A non-guilty verdict, Lord. Please!"), it was because there was a plan more suited to his higher purposes for our life. His perfect ways were ultimately leading to great gains spiritually, to practical lessons, and to priceless peace.

There was one more unforeseen bonus in this episode—a special gift from God that he knew would "knock my socks off." Pensacola is best known as the primary training base for all Navy, Marine, and Coast Guard aviators. It also serves as home base for the Navy Flight Demonstration Squadron, the Blue Angels. This precision-flying team practiced their jaw-dropping feats right over our large treeless backyard lawn.

Hearing their approach, I always stopped what I was doing to run outside. Gazing heavenward, my eyes would blur with tears of delight and wonder. I'd always been a bit obsessed with airplanes. This was pretty much known only to Bernie and the Lord. It might seem small to you, but to me it spoke once again—*How big is God!* While watching, I'd yell out, "Thanks, Lord, for sending Bernie to Eglin Federal Prison, Fort Walton Beach, Florida!"

CHAPTER 22

COMIC RELIEF

Bernie, meanwhile, wasn't the only one with a story about interesting accommodations. Mine may not have included a lock-down facility, but it did involve several lovely conference centers. Come with me for a behind-the-scenes glimpse of a speaker's life as she moves from one habitat to another.

Years ago I drove myself to a conference resort in Mississippi. I, the speaker, was glad for its proximity to Pensacola, since I wanted to take along a life-size stuffed dummy for the concluding presentation. Purchasing two airline tickets—one for her and one for me—would have been prohibitive.

The dummy was nicely outfitted and well behaved for the short trip. I checked into the hotel, drove my car around to my room, and seated soft, stuffed, prim and proper "Sally" on a chair near my bed before joining the retreat people for dinner. After I gave the evening message, I gave myself to the bed. A small problem presented itself: Outdoor lighting penetrated the curtains, illuminating the lady's realistic features just enough to unnerve me—Sally was staring at me! My tired mind's solution was to drape a thin scarf over her head. Now I could sleep—and if I rose before dawn, I wouldn't jump out of my skin on seeing her when I jumped out of bed.

Vacating my room in the morning to teach, I left Sally with her hands placed on the pages of a Gideon Bible, as I needed her to have a Bible for her grand entrance later. The flimsy scarf still veiled her face, since I continued to find her a bit eerie.

After lunch, the hotel manager spied me walking through the lobby, and he called me over. (He knew me by name because I was the speaker for the gathering.) As I stood with him, he exuberantly narrated the following story: That morning the housekeeper knew she was to clean the speaker's room. On seeing Sally, the maid thought it was Mrs. Reamer reposing in prayer. She asked if she might make the bed and change the towels. Mrs. Reamer didn't answer. She asked again and moved closer to the important person occupying the room. "Are you okay, Ma'am?" No answer. She touched the dummy's very life-like arm, but there was no sign of life. This young maid began to tremble and called the manager to inform him that the speaker, Mrs. Reamer, was dead. The manager and a desk clerk rushed to the room. They also received no response from poking Mrs. Reamer's arm or speaking loudly to her. Gloom filled the room. An important person had died! A person who could be used to change lives! The hotel exec bravely chose to remove the scarf ever so carefully . . .

Everyone shrieked in surprise and then happily sighed in relief. This "Mrs. Reamer" was just a dummy! The real one? Why, she's alive! And hopefully not a dummy.

As far as the hotel contingent was concerned, it was as if I had risen from the dead. This day, I was told, would go down as the happiest and most memorable in the history of the resort.

Another noteworthy event happened at a retreat in a picturesque wooded area in central Pennsylvania. A bit tired, I was facing a well-mannered, considerate crowd of women for my final teaching. But things were about to change . . .

I was nearing the end of the time allotted for my message, when alas!—a woman in an aisle seat leaped to her feet, screaming. Her panicked eyes gazed somewhere past my right shoulder. In mere seconds the room was filled with shrieking, running women! People were glancing somewhere beyond me as they made for the exit. Had a sniper entered from behind me? Or was there a bear from the thick woods about to pounce on me? (The rear wall was like one giant window, with sliding glass doors *that weren't locked.*)

It seemed as if no one cared that my life appeared to be in jeopardy; everyone was out to save her own. The "teaching diva" was forgotten. *Run for the hills. Don't look back!* the ladies seemed to be thinking; they didn't even take their Bibles, which were left in peril's path, along with me.

I followed my inclination . . . and joined with the screaming and running! As I bolted, I got as far as my microphone cord would allow. A loud BOOM sounded as the costly apparatus fell to the ground, adding an extra layer of "whodunit" to the pandemonium.

I noticed one person standing on a chair in the second row, looking frightened—and frightful! It was, of all people, Donna, the respected director of the retreat. *Jump on a chair, too*, I told myself, but there were none available since Bibles, purses, and other items occupied every seat. I ran to the director (who should have been my protector) and tried to climb onto her chair in order to reach a place of safety. I had one leg on the chair and the other dangling in the air as I kept urging her to move over a bit so I could get on. I began to scream out to anyone who had ears to hear, "What's happening!? What's wrong!?"

From somewhere came, "MOUSE!" and moments later, a few brave souls finally worked at ushering the "monster" outside. These courageous females were unsuccessful, so they built a maze out of book cartons to trap him. We all believed the mouse was somewhere in the maze. Eventually, all those who had fled returned to their chairs—and I, to the podium.

After a few minutes, screaming and running resumed, as the "scamperer" was back! The maze hadn't fazed Mighty Mouse. Donna hopped on her chair for the second time. Again, you would find me screaming and trying to stand with her on the shaky bridge chair, fighting for every inch of the seat. Those who had returned only minutes earlier ran for the hills a second time.

After ten minutes, with no more sightings of the troublesome creature, we resumed the meeting. And then my world came crashing down when the grey beast—now making its third appearance—nearly ran over my black patent pumps. I screamed louder this time, since I believed he had it in for me personally!

As I was dashing to the same chair amidst the same yells, the music leader grabbed my shoulders, trying to get me to turn around to see the rodent. She had no fear and wanted to show me how harmless the mouse was. I thought, *Are you really a female?* I almost socked her, as I needed for her to be elsewhere, and for me to be released from her clutches. With brute strength, I pulled away and again took to the chair. In the meantime, the management and kitchen staff upstairs heard the hysteria, and they figured the teacher (yours truly) was entertaining the attendees with some great stories.

The custodian came downstairs and rounded up the mouse with not one squeak . . . from the custodian, that is.

Calm finally returned. Apologetic, I humbly confessed I had not modeled what I'd been teaching right before the uninvited four-legged "whatchamacallit" had entered the room for the third time. The teaching: "We have two banks in our brains: a memory bank—what we *know* to be true; and an emotional bank—what we *feel* to be true. If our feelings don't line up with what we *know* to be true, we'd do well to discount them." I had then asked the ladies, "Where do you bank?" My teaching even included a command that occurs often, in one form or another, in the Bible: "Fear not! God is with you."

I had *felt* (in my emotional memory bank) that I was no match for the mouse. Neither did most of the other women. We believed a lie. At his first appearance, I had followed the crowd, not even knowing what the screaming and dashing around was about. That mouse would not have killed us or even brutally attacked us! But, somewhere in our collective *emotional memory bank* was this mathematical equation: Mice + women = chairs. There's an actual medical term for this phenomenon: *musophobia*. Bernie probably saw many mice in the dank prison. Did any of the men take to the chairs? Did anyone scream? Hardly.

As I closed the meeting, a woman raised her hand, wanting to share: "This was a perfect ending to your teaching, Judy. You come across as a confident woman of God, sure of his promises and so confident of his truth that you easily talk of casting down and casting out false beliefs. But enter a baby mouse, and you ran in the fear of the moment. As certain as you were of the principles you taught, you were afraid, and it's okay. It's normal to react *in the moment* and okay to be afraid. Everyone has her own mouse experience. God is still God, and a baby mouse is scary—for many."

Numerous times I find that what I teach is easier said than done. In my memory bank, where truth is stored, I knew no mouse would be out to kill me. I knew God—not a mini creature—is my protector and watches over me. (Though I must admit that my computer mouse does still know how to rattle me.)

Those two incidents ("The Dummy" and "The Fearsome Rodent") are just two of the occasions that have given me "something to write home about." Let me share one final example of how God sees to it that I'm never bored on the road or at any dwelling therein.

Have you ever been locked out of your hotel room? No big deal—you just go to the lobby and get a new key, right? Not in my case . . .

It was a few hours after the final afternoon session of a retreat at an upscale hotel in Huntsville, Alabama, and everyone from the event had left—except me. At 9 p.m., I called Bernie in Atlanta to say goodnight. It was rather early for me to bed down, but I had been fighting fatigue since the retreat's dismissal at 4 p.m.; for the next five hours I had to push myself to stay awake so I'd be able to sleep through the night.

When we hung up, I heard loud voices emanating from somewhere on my floor, and knew sleep wouldn't come because of the sheer volume. I thought, *If it's TV noise, the people will turn it off eventually and I'll wait it out, but if it's partiers, then I'll call the front desk.* (There had been a large wedding earlier in the ballroom, and a huge contingent from the celebration was rooming on my floor; if they were making the noise, I was afraid their revelry might last till the wee hours.)

Without thinking, I stuck my neck out the door to determine whether it was TV or a party. Since it still wasn't quite obvious enough, I walked one step farther. And while I was standing just inches from the threshold, the heavy door shut without so much as a "Good night, sweetheart." I thought since I had been speaking for God all weekend, maybe he would speak to the gold doorknob on my behalf and it would open. So I beseeched the Lord—but nothing changed.

An elevator might have taken care of the dilemma, but my attire wasn't appropriate for the ride: I had dressed for bed only minutes before, and since I travel as light as possible, my nightwear was . . . well, let's just say it was "nothing much to speak of." There was no way I was going to make a grand entrance into the lobby and risk arrest for unseemly garb! Maybe I could run down the fire escape from my high floor, but tripping was decidedly likely in my disoriented state. And what if the fire escape door somehow opened into the lobby? "You're under arrest, ma'am!"

As I stood outside my room in a near panic, I was sorely tempted to lower myself to the floor, assume fetal position, suck my thumb, and cry out, "I want my mommy!" Next, I (ridiculously) considered breaking down the door—but that would take fury, and all I felt was a fainting spell coming on. When an adrenaline surge failed to manifest, I came to my senses and realized I had to get my bare feet moving in some direction.

The hallways, with their colorful carpeting and handsomely framed wall pictures, were very long. I traversed them, listening in at every door to see if I could hear a woman's voice inside, as I wanted only a female to help me. All I could hear from the rooms, however, were TVs and men's voices. I wasn't about to knock on those doors and make a shocking dis*clothe*sure to them.

The only way I could navigate the halls without getting hysterical (as in sobbing) was to pretend I had no body—just a neck and a head. I talked myself into believing I was a bodiless human and found I could walk with my head held high. This lie kept me sane.

Fatigue was working overtime, along with my trauma and feelings of hopelessness. Yes, I was praying through it all. I looked for a hallway window, not to jump out, but to tear down the drapes so I could drape the fabric over my shivering—from nerves—body. Problem: There were no curtains, just venetian blinds!

At times, I hid in the alcove where the ice and vending machines were. It felt safe and became a prayer closet. "What am I to do, Lord?" During one of my walks down the hall, I heard the elevator door open. I dashed for the niche! A family was exiting the elevator. The little children spotted me huddled against the ice machine in my less-than-ideal outfit, so I held my index finger to my mouth, using the "Shush" gesture so they wouldn't alert their parents to look at this strangely clad woman. They obeyed me, for which I was thankful!

At one point, while hiding in the alcove, I took a peek out since I heard a loud, slurred voice coming from the far end of the corridor. I spotted a man in a tuxedo leaving one room and crossing the hallway into another. Desperation to bring this memorable night to a close caused me to step out from my safe haven.

The man saw me and stopped in his tracks. I didn't want to yell that I needed help for fear it would bring out more men from the wedding party (which I surmised from his tuxedo and inebriation). Motioning with my hand, I signaled him to walk towards me. When he got within talking distance, I instructed him, "Turn around backwards, please. Don't look at me!" When he complied, I spoke again. "I'm locked out of my room. Please go to the desk and tell someone."

He answered, "Okay," and once he left, it was a good ten minutes before I heard the elevator door open. I spent the time checking rooms again listening for a female and then hiding in the vending cave off and on. From that vantage point, I heard a little ding, indicating the elevator had stopped on my floor and saw two bellhops emerge. I stepped out from my hiding place and commanded firmly and quickly, "Turn around with your back to me! Have you come to help a woman who's locked out of her room?"

"Yes, Ma'am. Is it you?"

"It is. Do you have a key for me? If so, please hand me the key from behind your back."

As one of them did so, I grabbed the key with a hearty "thank you," opened my door, and fell on the bed, overcome with trauma from the ordeal.

I called Bernie and couldn't get the words out to tell him what happened. Every time I tried, I'd start crying again.

"Was it a roach?" (He knew how afraid I was of those two-inch Palmetto roaches in Florida and Alabama.)

"No!"

"Was it a mouse?"

"No!"

I finally was able to calm down enough to give him the details. He prayed for me and I collapsed into a deep sleep.

Early the next morning, when I got off the elevator and walked through the lobby, the two bellhops were there. They recognized me and asked how I was. How could they know me? I was now dressed in a conservative navy jacket and skirt with high heels, had on my makeup, and my hair was nicely coifed (compared to the earlier disheveled look). I appeared terribly proper. There was no resemblance to the woman they helped the night before. I didn't ask them how they knew me, but chose instead to exit the hotel pronto!

How ironic that my teaching for the nearby morning meeting was to be based on my book "Feelings Women Rarely Share" —about immorality, and sinfully using seduction to lure someone you can't have because he or you belong to someone else. One of my points was that women should dress modestly so as not to be a stumbling block to men. Did I practice what I preached? Shhhh!

Though it was anything but funny at the time, I can laugh now. The lesson from the story: It's fine to stick your neck out for others, but never stick your neck out a hotel room door.

I appreciate being able to share that and many other amusing memories from my years as a traveling teacher. Comic relief—oh, how I've needed it many times, and welcomed it in the midst of struggles. I wish I could've had some comic relief during my visit to what was, at the time, the largest hotel in the world. But there would be none during that adventure . . .

CHAPTER 23

JFR MEETS KGB (THE COMMITTEE FOR STATE SECURITY OF THE USSR)

There's a spiritual marker in the life of JFR (Judith Frances Reamer) that reinforced my belief in the existence of God. It's always good for me to think on such markers, because they fortify my appreciation for a God who is ever personal and has an individual plan for each of his children.

To begin this "marker" story, I must go back in time to a year after I returned from the life-changing Las Vegas trip. Bernie and I had decided to fly down to our condo in Hollywood, Florida. Our short stay coincided with a convention I was eager to attend. Bernie, in no relationship with God as yet, was not interested, but he was glad to escape the cold Maryland weather. Plus, we'd be able to have time to relax together.

The first night of the event, during an allotted time break between the two main speakers, a commonplace looking man was brought to the platform. He was introduced as a Bible smuggler whose dangerous journeys took him behind the Iron Curtain where Communism wielded a strong arm. His real name was not mentioned. Smuggling Bibles? What's that about?

"Bibles are forbidden in the Soviet Union." *They are?* He began to tell remarkable tales of Bibles making their way through checkpoints and other frightening obstacles. His life was in danger daily as were those who received the Bibles. The Scriptures were then divided into individual pages for distribution to hundreds of spiritually hungry individuals. People labored to memorize their page and then would trade it for another's page. My eyes began to sting and then tears began falling. However, when I glanced around, it appeared I was the only one visibly moved by the man's soul-stirring account. Why was I on the edge of my seat? Why was I transfixed by this courageous person?

The nameless man spoke twenty minutes. He told a few riveting stories about the persecution of Christians—how they lived in constant danger, how they were constantly being hunted down by the KGB, how they had to meet in great secrecy, and how precious a page of the Bible was to them. His description of the torture endured in Soviet prisons was painful. I found myself hurting terribly and hiding my eyes in several tissues.

From that time on, a great compassion gripped me for "The Suffering Church" of the USSR—for persons I had never met. This had to be a burden sovereignly birthed by the Lord. I began recognizing this burden as a divine assignment placed upon my life, just as with the smuggler. This was not born of my will.

Immediately, I began contributing as much money as possible to aid the smugglers in their life-risking mission. I also began secretly nurturing a yearning to carry Bibles into the Soviet Union myself. It was such an impossible prayer that I hadn't even told Bernie, although he was aware of my growing interest in the Soviet Union. I would have sold my home and given the money to provide help for the families whose husbands and fathers were languishing in prison for their faith. There was nothing I cared about more other than family. This continued for several years, during which time Bernie came to believe that Jesus was the promised Messiah when we were in California.

One day, to my astonishment, he called from the office. "Judy, how would you like to go with me to the Soviet Union?" I almost dropped the phone! It turned out that the Maryland State Bar Association was holding their conference behind the Iron Curtain that year. Strange! Communist Russia was a terrifying place. No one I knew ever chose to vacation there. And it would be unbearably frigid for the scheduled dates. But none of that mattered to me.

All I could think of was seizing this unforeseen opportunity to fulfill my sense of calling as a Bible courier. Realistically, I weighed the high risk of being caught and arrested at the airport with Bibles in my possession. But while giving ear to my fears, my heart would not be silenced. Over and over, I pondered what a few pages of the Bible could mean to a spiritually oppressed soul. I had no choice but to take the risk.

My preparations included tearing open the lining of my full-length, expensive winter coat and sewing many Bibles into it. Heavy, yes, but the burden was more so. I added Bibles to my luggage and Scripture leaflets to my boots.

Bernie and I decided he would not carry Bibles and risk arrest. After all, we had four children who needed at least one parent. Our flight landed in Moscow and I apprehensively joined the slow-moving luggage procession. I scrutinized the passengers ahead of me in the checkpoint line and cringed as their luggage was being searched. This was a terrible sign. All hope of escaping arrest was quickly evaporating. I was shaking in my boots when my turn came to pass through security. The inspectors glared at me, but did not open my suitcases! Of our large group of judges, lawyers, and spouses, I was the only one whose belongings went uninspected. *How big is God!*

Our hotel, the Rossiya, was the largest in the world and could accommodate 4,000. Gargantuan! Our room became a safe haven for me in the likewise gargantuan city. Outside the room, I knew I was facing danger since I was working to distribute the Bibles in a variety of ways, trusting God to providentially place them in the right hands. On the return trip, though I carried no Bibles, I had in my luggage some priceless antiquities handed to me by an old Russian Jew whose son, a former doctor, had escaped the Iron Curtain and was living in poverty in the United States. Like many other Jews, this formerly wealthy family had hidden a few treasures when Lenin swept through the land and confiscated their valuables and belongings. The treasures included two bottles of the son's favorite vodka! Those bottles were in the deep pockets of my winter coat.

So once again I stood in a customs line, this time at the Baltimore airport. Each passenger was asked the same questions. "Are you bringing any gifts that someone gave you while you were away? Are you bringing any antiques?" I knew I wouldn't lie, though I was shaking in the same boots again.

Once again God intervened on my behalf. As best I could tell, I was the only person in the long line who was not questioned! I passed right along, though my nerves clamored for strong drink. *Vodka, anyone?* I kiddingly whispered to Bernie that I was tempted to pull a bottle from my pocket!

The burden for the Iron Curtain countries remained in my heart even during the major relocation to Pensacola. I continued to send what little money I could, but would God send *me* back in person?

One night I had a strange dream in which I was at a Pensacola travel agency making arrangements for a trip. The name of the agency in my dream was "Fillette-Green." I had never heard such an odd name before, but in my dream a voice was speaking to me: "Do not forget this name." The voice was insistent. In my dream I kept repeating "Fillette-Green" so as to remember it, with no awareness it was happening during a sound sleep.

The next morning I needed to make a call. Above the wall phone, months earlier, I had tacked a calendar the size of a business card. I couldn't tell you where I got it. When I picked up the phone, the card fell to the floor . . . after all this time. I reached down to retrieve it and stopped short. On the flip side of the calendar were the words: Fillette-Green Travel Agency—specializing in travels to the *Soviet Union* and Scandinavian countries. Wonder of wonders! Here we go with this big God again!

I placed a call to my close friend Pat (not Boone!) in Pennsylvania, asking her to travel to Russia with me. She accepted and I booked flights through Fillette-Green, the experts on Russian travel. Our purpose would be to help those who were suffering under Communist rule. The Soviet religion was atheism. Imprisonment was certain for those found worshiping God. I had some names and addresses of those who were living in misery, suffering for their faith. We would find them . . .

The week before our departure from New York, I was to speak at a conference in Pittsburgh where a Bible smuggler was also on the program. While there, he and I were invited to do a live TV interview.

On the air Steve, the smuggler, described a recent trip to the Soviet Union. I added I was on my way there, Monday, a week from then. It never occurred to me that the KGB (who had been following this man for years) was watching that program, and thus heard me announce my plans.

The following Monday at the airport in New York, Pat and I approached the ticketing counter of Finnish Airlines. We had arrived three hours earlier to get a two-seat configuration in order to pray privately on the long flight. (This was before people could pre-book seats.)

The Finn behind the counter gruffly told us there were none left. We would have to sit in the five-seat middle area. She would not give in, though we could see the seating chart showed plenty of our seat preference not yet assigned. We returned to the waiting area baffled by the ticketing agent and her refusal to give us what we wanted.

When we returned to the waiting area to sit down, two women came up and sat beside us. They began engaging us in conversation, telling us, with heavy Russian accents, that they lived in New Jersey and were going to visit relatives in Russia.

We finally boarded the plane, which held over three-hundred passengers. To our surprise, these very same women were seated next to us. Pat and I began to be uneasy. Had the KGB sent two female agents to tail us, to try to get information from us? They obviously had been seated with us in the middle section. We knew the Finnish airline agent in New York was most likely working with the KGB. (At the time many in Finland were active members of the Communist party.)

"I want to go home!"

"Me too!"

Pat and I were whispering fearfully to one another. The plane was now airborne. There was no turning back. "Oy vey, Pat! I am so sorry I got you into this!" I had in my purse the names and addresses of persecuted families we were planning to contact. I leaned over to her. "Let's go to the lavatory—NOW!"

There in the tiny bathroom we talked and prayed. Who were we to think we could survive in the middle of enemy territory—in the USSR? When we got back to our seats, I noticed that my large tote bag had been moved and opened.

Shaken, I excused myself again. I returned to the bathroom, took the list of persecuted people from my purse, tore the paper into small pieces and trashed them. I could not put these precious people at risk. My heart was unspeakably sad. *And* how much risk were Pat and I taking?

We changed planes in Finland and the women were once again seated next to us! We could have moved to empty seats on either plane. "It will raise more suspicion," Pat warned. So we sat with these scary characters. It was like something out of a spy movie. Pat and I were starring in it! *This is not a dream, Judy. This is happening real time!* We were shaken and praying fervently in silence. The trip had barely gotten under way . . .

CHAPTER 24

A PUSHY ANGEL

I wasn't surprised to find the two women assigned to the room next to us after we checked into the enormous Rossiya Hotel in Moscow hotel—a repeat accommodation for me. We were traveling in a tour group booked by the Fillette-Green travel agency. Casually, I asked our guide if anyone had signed up at the last minute. "Yes, two women booked a reservation only a week ago." Aha! It had been a week since I had done the TV show.

In our room, Pat and I played music tapes as loudly as we dared. This ploy allowed us to pray together and discuss options. We assumed our room was bugged. Since both of us were fun-loving by nature, we decided we would role-play to confuse the two agents. Pat would be chatty and outgoing; I would act shy and aloof. She'd keep the women busy with much chatter, engaging them in long conversations, while I, the stand-offish, non-conversational one, would more easily be able to get away, albeit alone. That was hugely unsettling, but I knew what to do with the accompanying emotions. Cast them on the perfect Protector! Why should both of us worry?

One of my solo ventures was to get into the *Museum of History of Religion and Atheism* in St. Petersburg. It served as the headquarters of a militant organization whose purpose was not merely to disparage God but literally to deny His existence. No Bible smugglers I knew of were able to get in to determine what was inside. The Museum was housed in what once was a grand Russian Orthodox cathedral— Kazan Cathedral. The former church was now being used to persuade people that science has taken the place of religion.

Pat and I devised a plan that would allow me to "escape" the tour, going off alone to find the Museum of Atheism. On a train ride across the Russian countryside, I mentioned to our KGB female companions that I was an art teacher. "I cannot wait to visit the famous Hermitage Art Museum in St. Petersburg," I told them. "I'm fascinated by the Russian dynasties and want an opportunity to view artifacts from that period."

The next morning I remained in the hotel room while Pat and the two women boarded the tour bus for a former Czar's palatial home. Pat explained to our group leader that because of my profession, I wanted to spend a good deal of time visiting the extensive painting collection of the Hermitage instead of the palace. This, of course, upset the spies. Since the two were to be with me whenever I left my room, this upset them, and they insisted Pat go get me.

Pat returned to our room. "Judy, they're insisting that you get on that bus. The driver said he'll drop you off at the Hermitage." I knew the agents wanted to see that I actually went to the Hermitage so they could notify someone to keep an eye on me. Not wanting to go to the world-famous art museum but having no choice, I boarded the bus and was dropped off at the Hermitage. What to do now? Assuming a notice would go out to track me in the museum, I needed a plan.

It turned out to be very easy to get lost in the stunning Hermitage. The place is monstrous in size! I dashed and darted through the hallways and alcoves of the mammoth building. I stopped to stare for five minutes at "The Return of the Prodigal Son" by Rembrandt, truly wanting to reflect on the monumental masterpiece for an hour, but I needed to stay on course. Outwardly I appeared to know where I was going and what I was doing, but inwardly I was holding on to God for dear life. Then suddenly I spotted a door that led outside.

Stepping into the cold, drizzly, gray afternoon, I pulled out my map and found the subway terminal. Because all the signs were written in Russian, I was worried I'd get off at the wrong stop. So I counted the stations on my map. There were nine of them. I also happened to have nine buttons on my raincoat. Moving my finger from button to button as I rode from stop to stop, I was able to get off at the right station.

The former Kazan cathedral that housed the museum was both magnificent and enormous, filling an entire city block. It wrapped around in a large semi-circle, with long rows of columns. The central dome was an imitation of St. Peter's in Rome. I was awestruck!

A very long line of people, bundled in heavy clothes, shivered as they waited to get in. By now it was 4:00 p.m. Suddenly the front doors opened and a guard came out. He shouted something in Russian, which I gathered meant "No more people in! We're closing! Leave!" The people who had waited so long were clearly angry. Eventually, in small groups, they headed back toward the subway. I, too, was extremely discouraged. God had brought me here from halfway around the world. I had truly believed he wanted me to pray for the fall of Communism in this very building.

As I slowly turned to join the others, an old Russian woman approached me from out of nowhere. Suddenly she wrapped her arm in mine and began to tug me toward the museum. I was terrified! *Think. Think, Jude—how do you say "No"?*

"Nyet! Nyet!" I shouted at her. I pointed to my watch as if I had to be somewhere else. I tried to pull away. But she was very strong, and she would not let me go. I was scared. She dragged me around to the back of the gargantuan building, where she banged on a door, and a guard appeared. The old woman said something to him, pressed some coins into my hand, and pushed me through the door.

I caught my breath and looked around. In a small booth sat a cashier who was evidently collecting the fee required to tour the museum. It had never occurred to me that I might need to pay before entering. I held out the coins in my hand, which turned out to be the exact amount.

I was placed in a small group of maybe fifteen people, to which a tour guide was assigned. I heard German and French in my group, but no one was speaking English. We began to move through the building. The Marxist Soviet Union devoted itself to the demolishing of religious beliefs and to the propagation of atheism. I was in its central headquarters!

Soon I pulled away from the group and went off by myself. I honestly don't know what I was expecting to see, but there are no words to describe the horror of that place. It was as though I had stepped into the halls of hell. What I saw was grotesque, revolting, and unspeakable. There may have been other religions represented, but the pictures I saw were all viciously directed at Christianity.

The deliberate agenda was the total destruction of all religious faith in the country. How was I to reconcile my awe, inspired by the grandeur of the former cathedral, with my disgust and revulsion, produced by the rows of anti-religious exhibits? I stared in shock at the giant lewd murals stretched across entire walls. In each picture, there was a Christ figure, identifiable by the blood pouring from his hands. His face was contorted into the most evil expressions. I do not want to tell you what I saw in the murals. For me, it was worse than viewing hard-core pornography. I wanted to cover my eyes, fall to the floor, and weep.

But of course I couldn't. So I prayed for the Soviet Union. I prayed for the persecuted Jewish people. I prayed with all that was within me for the fall of Communism. The Spirit of God gave me prayers I couldn't even understand, flowing out of my innermost being as I spent time in rooms by myself.

After the museum closed about an hour later, I stumbled back to the subway and somehow made it to our hotel. The women in the next room had lots of questions about the Hermitage. My abrupt response was mere politeness. "It was good. Very crowded, though."

It was about a year later when the mighty edifice of Communism began to crumble. Within five years the Soviet Union itself was dissolved into a number of independent countries, and both Jews and Christians were again able to have Bibles and worship God without government restraint. It was one of the happiest moments of my life when the wall came down in Berlin.

Today, as I reflect upon the providential workings of God that enabled me to participate in that miracle, I marvel. The wonder of how he used the prayers of thousands to break strongholds of seemingly impenetrable evil in the Soviet Union. To be a participant with God was awesome.

Now the eleven-time-zone land mass encasing Russia and other countries like Ukraine (once part of the USSR) is once again in the middle of troublesome, frightening days. I am thankful for the window that opened up years ago but realize the future is uncertain for the land my grandparents once called home. Whenever I hear the Russian national anthem during the Olympics, my eyes get teary. Is it deep calling unto deep? Maybe that is why I have an inordinate love for snow, for winter storms. And maybe that's the reason the Lord knew I wouldn't be resistant to the assignment he gave me.

CHAPTER 25

BREAKING THE BIBLE BARRIER

The newfound joy I had for the Russian people was in knowing they now had access to the Scripture. One problem: Bibles were few in number. Pages had to be torn out and passed around, allowing those who had never seen God's Word to view it, even if just one page at a time until another came along.

Meanwhile, back in the democratic United States, multitudes of homes had multitudes of Bibles. Anybody could have access to one—even in hotel rooms. Soon I would discover that whether a home had one Bible or fifteen, the majority of homeowners were not reading, not applying, not interested in this holy collection of writings. The three pivotal reasons Bibles were gathering dust in homes:

1. "I don't have time to read anything of that size."
2. "I'm not 'brainy' enough to tackle the scope of its meaning."
3. "I'll go to my pastor/rabbi for answers."

Sadly, those were my reasons, too.

One weekend, while teaching at a large retreat, I began to feel sorry for the attendees. Tears had been flowing because my topic had been rather convicting. I was certain tears would turn to joy by retreat's close on Sunday, but this was only Saturday. After lunch I was about to embark on the next teaching in the series and thought, *Everyone needs a fun break. I think I'll play a joke.*

"Let's begin the session by going to the book of Obadiah, chapter one." I had to work hard to keep from laughing as I watched the group rifle through the Bible. I was rather enjoying the sight of the impossible search. After a minute or so I noticed one person after another had stopped flipping pages and was making eye contact with me. No one was flashing a smile or giving me a wink. There was no indication they were thinking, *We get the joke, O Most Funny Lady!*

The people were looking as temperate as if I had asked them to turn to Genesis, chapter one—the easiest book to find since it's the first. I slowly sobered up when I realized there really *was* a book named Obadiah!

Oy vey, Judy, what a matzo-ball you are. I thought Obadiah was the name of someone in the begats or a Pharaoh's daughter . . . not a book of the B-I-B-L-E! I was mortified and prayed, *Dear God, if You get me out of this, I'll pack my suitcases tomorrow and fly to Africa and serve the Mau-Mau tribe all the days of my life! Just help me save face!* I glanced at the clock on the wall and said aloud, "Wow! I didn't realize how late it was, so let's pass over Obadiah and turn to the book of Isaiah, chapter twenty-seven." *Thank You, God, for the idea. You saved me!* No one caught my error—and this detail was wondrous in my sight.

It's funny to think about it now, but in spite of the fact that I'd exhaustively researched and studied many different subjects in Scripture, the hard truth was, I had been in national public ministry for *twelve years* and *had never read through my Bible once.* No one knew.

Because unfamiliarity with the Scriptures is so common, I surmise there are those who think Abraham, Isaac, and Jacob may have had a few hit songs during the '60s. How about those who think there's a story in the Bible about Jonah the shepherd boy and his ark of many colors? Maybe even some who would declare Hercules to be their favorite Old Testament patriarch. How about wondering if the *Minor* Prophets worked in the quarries? Maybe even I did . . . but I'm not owning up.

When I returned home from the retreat, I decided to "quit" teaching others about God until I became familiar with the whole Bible. I made my "problem" a matter of prayer. I found myself desperately desiring to be a Bible reader, not to impress others or myself. I realized Scripture offers the one clear peek into who God is. That's what drew me. There were historic people who wrote of him, who were said to know his heart and mind. About forty people in the Bible wrote their stories about God. Was there agreement on what God was like? I didn't want to ignore any of those writers.

My New Year's resolutions always included a determination to read the entire Bible. I'd start out reading Genesis in January. Where was I at year's end? Truth be told, not very far. One of the main reasons I never made it through was the "studier" in me wouldn't allow for skipping a passage without gaining an understanding. I'd pull out a Concordance that has every word in Greek or Hebrew, then a Bible dictionary and also a couple of commentaries. I'd get stuck in the more complex passages (after all, there are some strange things in the Bible!). I could never catch the whole counsel of God because I wasn't far from Genesis at year's end.

For instance, I would get to the list of offerings in Leviticus—sin offerings, burnt offerings, fellowship offerings, wave offerings. These were required of the Israelites to be in right standing with their God. Wanting to delve into the full meaning of what I was reading, I'd feel guilty (though it was false guilt) if I skipped or ignored anything. So, this was one New Year's resolution that took flight every year.

I imagined there were readers who considered the offerings irrelevant so they would move to Bible portions deemed easier to comprehend—the Book of Proverbs (there are thirty-one proverbs, which serve well for a month's reading and can be repeated twelve times a year). Or maybe just reading Psalms would assuage any guilt. The Jewish apostle Paul wrote in a letter that *all* Scripture is God-breathed and useful for teaching, rebuking, correcting and training in righteousness, so that those who love God may be well equipped for every life situation. Because of what he wrote, I wanted to see the *whole* of Scripture. I wanted to use the Word of God rather than the self-help manuals on my shelf as a roadmap for life.

What was happening to me during those first twelve years of Bible teaching? Well, I was depending on preachers to take the place of my Bible. If you would have asked, "Are you a Bible reader, Judy?" I'd have answered, "Oh, yes." The reality was that I was reading just a Proverb or Psalm a day and I'd maybe read from the book of Esther or Jonah, stories I was familiar with from Sunday school days.

It followed that any preacher who could give me three verses, along with a poem or a story, to prove his theology was credible to my way of thinking. I was eating pre-chewed food. I could never challenge any teaching because I had no biblical foundation.

Here's the wonderful story of how all that changed: "Hey, Mom!" my son Johnny yelled as he came in the door after school. "A man named Phillip Green came to school today who's read the Bible 12,000 times! I brought you a brochure about him. He's known as the walking Bible and is in the *Guinness World Book of Records.*"

I thought, *This man is a wonder! I can't even get through the Bible once.* That night after everyone had gone to bed, I read the pamphlet. A week later, after just seven days of following Green's suggestions, I was at the beginning of the book of Judges. I found that remarkable. One-fourth of the Bible was completed. I was "seeing" God on every page and taking in so many of his thoughts at one time that my faith started to skyrocket.

When the week ended, something else made me marvel. On a trip to a local shopping plaza, walking out of a store, I literally bumped into a couple of friends who were accompanied by a short black-haired gentleman who resembled a cuddly teddy bear.

When they introduced us with "Judy, this is Phillip Green," I thought my eyes would pop right out of my head. "Phillip Green!" I squealed. "Are you the man who's read the Bible 12,000 times?" Yes. Same one.

This man had traveled around the world eight times, engaging people in Bible reading. Sixty-six countries! He was in town to lead a series of meetings, which I eagerly attended.

As I sat under his wise counsel, at meetings and in private, I discovered there should be three parts to the time we set aside to be alone with God. I knew about the first two—praying and studying. Phillip taught me about the third: reading.

Just reading! Not study time, not prayer time. But reading exactly as I'd read a novel. This was easy—I didn't have to *do* anything but read, I could just read and soak in *whatever God chose to open up for me.* Phillip told me of a survey he'd taken from around the world when he did research on Bible reading. The report showed that ninety-eight percent of those who had chosen to follow God's will had never read through the Bible one time. In fact, ninety percent of pastors in pulpits fall into the same category! So I wasn't alone.

Phillip went on to say that the Bible, with estimated annual sales of twenty-five million copies, has been a major influence on literature and history, especially in the West where it was the first mass-printed book. Here are a few more of the many things I learned from this very special man:

1. A major reading institute in America teaches that you will retain only twenty percent of what you read, whether you are a fast or slow reader. The purpose of reading, and maybe quickening your usual pace, is to have a spiritual foundation built on the *whole* Bible. Each time through the Bible, the percentage of retained comprehension builds up. Enjoy what you do understand, knowing God will open up more and more each time through.

2. Since God primarily speaks from Scripture, the more the eye-gate sees, the broader the base he has from which to speak to us. If we're reading only Proverbs and Psalms, that is all God has to draw from when he wants to impact our thoughts in any given situation or relationship.

3. Reading is *not* a substitute for studying, but getting people to study is quite a task in contrast to motivating them to read. In the book of Luke, it was Jesus who opened up the Jewish Scriptures to the Israelites. They needed to be familiar with Scripture, to have read it, even if they didn't always catch the meaning at first. It was the Messiah who marvelously took what they read and simply explained the significance. God does the same for us today as we read. He illuminates the verses to those who desire his will.

Because of Phillip Green's unique plan, my entire family discovered the inexhaustible Bible. It was no longer a foreboding, too-difficult-to-handle dust collector. One of my children read through the Bible four times in one year at age twelve. There was no intimidation since the children were asked just to read, and they knew the Lord would take the responsibility to cause something to "pop" off the page just for them.

Bernie and I knew it would be beneficial, since we were sure that our reading materials were more than just words printed on paper. In my case, what happened is that the Bible became more than just a collection of manuscripts written centuries ago. It's where I met with God; it's where he and I had conversations. Reading through my Bible was worth nothing if there was no impact. I didn't need more facts; I needed to be more loving (and certainly still do). But what those inspired men of yesteryear wrote—their God-breathed writings—impacted my words, my thoughts, my actions more than anything else in my life did. More than Pat Boone—and that's saying a whole lot!

I've heard it said: "Remember it's not how many times you go through the Bible, but do you humbly submit to allow the Scriptures to go through you?" My thought was, *I don't understand how a person can remain untouched once they begin to get into the Bible.*

I think author Chris Webb answered my question: "Sometimes, of course, the reason is very simple: resistance. We don't want to be changed. As soon as the Bible begins to challenge us, to undermine our prejudices and dogmas, to call for a change in our lifestyle and priorities, then the shutters slam down" (*The Fire of the Word,* IVP Press).

I have thanked God over and over for answering my prayer concerning the "problem" of not knowing how best to experience his whole counsel. Oh, the *wonder* of providentially meeting Phillip Green! *How big is God!*

Phillip Green died at age ninety-two in 2001, having read the Bible numerous more times than when I first met him. Phillip lost his eyesight days before he died, yet as he lay on his bed, the Bible was propped on his chest and he'd turn its pages. His daughter asked, "Daddy, what are you doing?" "I'm reading my Bible," he replied. He had seen the pages so many thousands of times that when he turned from one to the next, starting in Genesis, he knew what was written there.

At this point in time, I am benefiting from being in a "sorta" book club—the book being the Bible. There's a wonderful vibrancy, with much richness discussing what God has revealed to each one. God can reveal different facets or applications of his unchanging truth, depending on each individual's unique personality and circumstance. We're all on the same pages (that is, pages of the Bible) but not necessarily "on the same page" as we have insights that may differ on tough questions. I am amazed how the dynamic of a group setting builds and strengthens us individually and as a community—one composed of believers who want to be followers of God and not just "fans" of his. This is happening through the unifying power of his story.

Though I now am a book club "groupie," I remain an introvert at heart. (When I'm outside the confines of home, you wouldn't think so.) My preference would be to sit and learn through reading and research all day long. I fall into the category of people who need coaxing to leave the house. There's another category of people that is the opposite. These persons enjoy going "hither and thither" and have little desire to remain still or live in isolation. Regarding the Bible, I thought this poem addressed both categories—me as well as what is probably the majority of the population. The first two lines point to me; the last two lines—the extroverts.

If I do a lifetime of reading the Bible, *without*
living,
I'll never know if what I read is true,
But if I do a lifetime of living, *without* the Bible,
I'll never know with living what to do.
(Author unknown)

(For details on the "hows and whys" of my favorite Bible
reading plan, please visit: judyreamer.com.)

CHAPTER 26

"I WILL TAKE HIM AWAY."

If Bernie said it once, he said it a hundred times: "I'd move from Pensacola if two of the children ever lived in the same city."

We were in the full swing of empty nesting. The four children had departed for college and were concerned about what Bernie and I were going to do without any of them around. He quipped, "I'm going to be chasing your mother around the house!" We all laughed, but I knew Bernie was thinking about what he had always said. Since two of the boys settled in Atlanta after college, Bernie was thrilled when he was able to procure a job in Georgia, where "some" children could be hugged regularly.

Bernie was a great father, and when the Atlanta boys, Mark and Jeff, were married (not to each other!) and had children, he was great at grandfathering too. Another married son, Johnny, lived in St. Louis, and our daughter Jill (Jeff's twin), who lived in Tulsa, was engaged. All was at peace in our world.

One February evening I was pacing the floor, praying in my home office. (When I pray, pacing seems like the natural accompaniment.) At the moment, Bernie was my focus. I had just entered the library and was about two feet from my bookcase when I was stopped in my tracks by five words that were not my own—*I WILL TAKE HIM AWAY.* My blood chilled. I was numbed. The room's furnishings lost all color, and I saw only grays, blacks, and whites.

Maybe I heard wrong. "If this is You, Lord, please repeat the words." *I WILL TAKE HIM AWAY.* I heard the exact five words again! This was one of the most unnerving moments of my whole life. And then I heard, *TELL NO ONE.* "No one? Not Bernie?" *NO ONE.* (The words were not spoken audibly, but I heard them with an uncanny, unexplainable knowing—which is part and parcel of intimacy with the Lord. I recognized that this was what the Bible describes as the "still, small voice" of God.)

As the days passed, I dismissed those five words since my husband showed no evidence of ill health, and I'd heard nothing more from God. One unusually warm late-winter day, Bernie and I were enjoying a leisurely walking outdoors. A cozy feeling wafted over my being at the thought of us still going for walks, holding hands like this, in our eighties.

Immediately, I heard that same inaudible but real voice: "You and Bernie will not be walking hand in hand together in your eighties. *I WILL TAKE HIM AWAY.*" The tone of God's voice was not harsh or condemning or threatening. They were words that God, in His goodness, needed me to hear—for his purposes later on. In hindsight, the words remind me of how a parent would speak to a child who's swimming when thunder sounds. *With no need to be flowery*, the parent would speak in a straightforward manner to provide loving direction: "I am taking you inside."

Though I was disarmed once more, when Bernie and I finished our walk, I again dismissed *I WILL TAKE HIM AWAY.* There was no reason to keep those words "on the front burner" since life was busy, busy, busy and happy, happy, happy.

But then . . . but then . . . but then, in April, Bernie mentioned his stomach was hurting him. The ache was dull, and he wrote it off as just common discomfort. A week later Bernie told me he was losing weight. Because I saw him daily, I hadn't detected the loss, but the scale had taken notice. I wrote it off with, "Bernie, you're a great tennis player. Isn't it normal to lose weight when playing a lot of tennis? Now that spring's here, you've been on the courts a lot."

But then . . . but then . . . but then, his pain was increasing, his weight dropping more. In late May, Bernie went to the doctor and underwent test after test. It wasn't an ulcer; nor was it a gall bladder problem. Meanwhile, our only daughter was in the midst of planning a July wedding in Tulsa. With the details of her big day rising to the top of our priority list, self-sacrificing Bernie barely mentioned his growing distress. Arriving in Tulsa a few days before the wedding, I had no idea how much my husband was hurting.

It was a dream wedding, and Bernie contributed royally as the ideal father of the bride. But during those days in Tulsa, every time we returned to our hotel room, he would lie down in pain. I could see it in his contorted face.

With Jill and Terry honeymooning, we returned to Atlanta and a gastroenterologist scheduled a biopsy. After the procedure, Bernie was transferred to a hospital bed while awaiting the doctor's report. I sat silently by him. He wasn't himself and didn't want to talk. The surgeon walked in, and his words were, "Go home and get everything together, Bernie. I am so sorry. You have, at the most, six months to live."

The announcement paralyzed us both for a moment. We couldn't move; we didn't respond. We just stared at the man in the white coat. The news was surreal, dreamlike. "Bernie, you have pancreatic cancer. There's one large tumor, which is inoperable. Chemotherapy and radiation are not options either. There's nothing to be done."

I drove Bernie home, only to have our world turned into visiting health stores, attending seminars for alternative cancer treatments, and doing so much research that we felt like experts on his particular condition.

Bernie was determined to beat this thing. He thought he would be healed by God, or at least by all the natural supplements and concoctions which made him gag. People all over the country were praying, and we attended many prayer services for healing.

With all this happening to Bernie, what was happening with *me*? My main activity was tossing and turning at night. "I will never be able to fall asleep, dear Lord, until you tell me if the five words—*I WILL TAKE HIM AWAY*—are upon me. If you will just tell me, I will know whether Bernie is going to die. I don't know whether to accept as inevitable what the doctor told us. I need to know, God!" But I received no answer. I knew of the Lord's goodness and love for me, so I trusted that "Father knows best," even though I desperately wanted a "Yes" or "No."

I also struggled with not being able to share the words with Bernie. God had impressed on me—*NO ONE*. I would not be disobedient to what I knew was his directive. The future regrets I'd have for sharing the "secret" would undoubtedly be far more unsettling than my present plight.

Bernie made a decision to go to Memphis for a procedure that made use of a technology known as Radiofrequency Thermal Ablation (RiTA, for short—which is pronounced "ritta"). Dr. Roy Page, a renowned surgical oncologist, was one of the few surgeons in the country who was using the RiTA machine. He had great success with the simple procedure and assured us it would take just fifteen minutes to "fry the tumor." Once inside the body, the machine's prongs open up, grab the tumor, and fry it. No side effects, no surgical scarring. After being used successfully in Italy for years, the FDA had finally approved it for the USA.

There was nobody but me in the huge waiting area of the outpatient medical center—other than a woman on the far side. I spotted a bay window with a cushioned seat. Taking out my Bible, I sat at the window with the sun pouring in. After several minutes of reading and praying, I looked up to see a plainly attired woman standing before me. I recognized her as the one from the other side of the room. I had no desire to converse with her, but instead desperately wanted to use the next forty-five minutes to pray for my husband.

With an unmistakable Southern accent, she asked, "Is your husband in for the RiTA procedure with Dr. Page?"

"Yes, my husband is in surgery now."

"My son will follow your husband for the same procedure. We come from Appalachia, from the mountains of Virginia."

"Oh," I nodded, unsmiling.

Please, go back to where you were in the room. I need time alone.

But she didn't move. And then . . .

"In February 1986 a doctor pulled me aside at the Veterans Hospital where my husband was getting a biopsy for cancer. He said 'Get everything fixed up.' I knew the doctor was pronouncing the final days of my husband's life. I went home and talked with God, asking him to indicate what month my husband would die. Mentioning each month in turn, when I got to August, I heard the words, *Monte Vista.* Immediately I recalled this as the cemetery where my husband and I had funeral plots. He died the last of *August.* God does speak to me about things to come, and I felt impressed to tell you about this experience."

She then turned and walked away, having uttered not another word. At first I thought her to be really strange. *She had walked over only to share about her husband's death?* I was befuddled. What would motivate the lady to bother me with this? Why should I care? It didn't fit.

I decided to rehearse her words. When I got to her mentioning the month of *August* and then her hearing *Monte Vista*, I paused. She'd heard a voice from heaven, announcing her husband's impending demise. Slowly it sank in that this plain Appalachian woman's story was related to my question: "Lord, is this the time the five words—*I WILL TAKE HIM AWAY*—are upon me?"

The woman's "visit" was convincing me to accept what I had heard from God in February—and to accept what I was to hear next from that still, small voice: *YES. THIS IS THE TIME WHEN I WILL TAKE BERNIE AWAY. THE TIME IS VERY SHORT. THIS IS THAT WHICH I SPOKE TO YOU MONTHS AGO.*

From this point on, I would no longer need to plead with God to tell me whether Bernie's sickness was an affliction unto death. I was at peace.

Dr. Page came out to tell me how pleased he was with the procedure. Ninety-five percent of the large tumor was gone! There was no incision, and the remaining five percent would be taken care of with minor radiation. When Bernie came out of recovery, he was so encouraged. But I now knew, in spite of the doctor's words, my husband was going to die.

Dr. Page asked Bernie and me to stay in a motel over the weekend so he could check him if needed. Right after midnight, I was aware Bernie was trying to get out of the bed. I assumed he was headed for the bathroom, not knowing he was delirious with a high fever. When Bernie stood up, he collapsed and fell to the floor.

I called the front desk for help and learned that the employee manning the desk was the only staff person left at the small motel. He came up to the room, took one look at Bernie and announced, "We are going to the hospital. I'll get a wheelchair." After transporting Bernie's inert body to the man's car, we took off for the emergency room.

The results from Bernie's tests indicated the setback was not from cancer or the RiTA procedure. Instead, he had a severe blood infection called sepsis, which can lead to organ failure and death. The infectious disease doctor showed up to determine what antibiotic treatment to start. He was hopeful they'd find the right one to fight the staph infection, but I wasn't. God again reminded me to tell no one.

CHAPTER 27

THE FIVE WORDS COME TO PASS

Gradually, Bernie's high fever dissipated. Mark, Johnny, Jeff, and Jill had traveled to join me in Memphis, but when the crisis appeared to pass, everyone but Jill left for home. Bernie had been moved from the ICU to a regular floor. On entering his new room, I spotted a rendering of Jesus's face on a paper tacked to the bulletin board. The message above the image read, "Good morning! This is God. I will be handling all your problems today. I will not need your help, so have a good day. I love you!"

I knew that every hospital room gets swept clean of all personal effects from the previous patient. Nothing is left in drawers, on walls, or on shelves. I thought, *How nice that all the rooms have these encouraging words to view daily.* (It was a Catholic hospital, so I understood why there would be a picture representing Jesus.)

But a short while later, as I was taking a walk down the hall, I happened to notice the bulletin board in another patient's room, and there was no picture of Jesus. Curious, I peeked into every room on that floor. Bernie's was the only one with what I now realized was God's personal direction for me: "I will be handling all your problems today. I will not need your help so have a good day."

Bernie began to go downhill. Doctors were unable to find an antibiotic potent enough to strike a deathblow to the infection. For the last three days of his life, Jill and I stayed by his side and kept in touch constantly with the three boys who'd just gone home. At 7:30 in the morning, after a night of unspeakable suffering for Bernie, the medical staff came running. The doctor on call said, "This is the end. Do you wish us to keep him alive or not?"

Jill and I were sobbing. Does God want us to keep him alive in a vegetative state, or should we let him die? *What's the right decision?* A small, balding man in a gray suit was coming towards us from the other end of the long corridor. "I am the hospital chaplain. I see you women are distressed. May I help you?"

"The doctor tells me my husband is dying, and now it's up to me whether to use artificial means to keep him alive. I don't know what to do. My name is Judy and this is Jill, our daughter."

"Does your husband have a living will?

A light went on in my soul. "Yes! Yes!"

And I knew what Bernie had wanted. "Then it's not your decision to make, Judy. Your husband has made the decision for you. He does not want to be kept alive with a ventilator."

I wanted to hug this God-sent messenger. In my confusion, it hadn't dawned on me to think of the living will. Bernie was being moved back to Intensive Care, so Jill and I went there to await his arrival. The ICU nurse told us death was close. At this moment, I heard the heavenly voice again: *NOW TELL BERNIE WHAT I SPOKE TO YOU.*

I leaned over and talked into Bernie's ear. The nurse had said he couldn't speak but could still hear. "The last thing to go is the hearing." So I told him every detail of what I had held in my heart since that February day. The last thing I said into his ear was, "Relax and let go. I ask you to forgive me for anything wrong I have done to you, and I forgive you for anything wrong you have done to me." (I've shared with many the benefit of speaking those words to a dying loved one who no longer can communicate. Doing so helps after the person is gone: The slate is clean between you.)

Jill and I kept encouraging Bernie to hang on, as the rest of the family was on its way, some traveling a long distance. While we waited for them to arrive, Jill reminded Bernie of great times and kidded him about his funny foibles. It took twelve hours for everyone to reach the hospital, but they all were able to say goodbye to their darling dad. The children managed to make it from St. Louis and Atlanta, and Jill's husband Terry also got in from Tulsa. Bernie's mother, brother, and sister had arrived earlier.

The ICU nurse kept expressing amazement that Bernie was able to hold on for so long. Death was supposed to have come twelve hours earlier. *How big is God!*

The grands talked to their beloved "Grandpa Bernie" as we held the phone close to his ear. Grandpa's lips were silent, but tears ran down from his closed eyes. The nurse told us, "Even though he can't speak, keep on talking to him." We sang hymns and praise songs and talked non-stop to him.

On seeing the heart monitor flat-line, the nurse informed us Bernie had just passed away, surrounded by a loving family. I was sobbing. The ICU nurse pulled me aside and said, "Judy, it's hard to believe this now, but although Bernie died within nine weeks of the cancer diagnosis, he went quickly. I've been an ICU nurse for eleven years and have seen cancer patients come in and out of ICU. The emotional and physical toll it takes on the patient and family is huge. Really, Judy, in hindsight, you will be glad he didn't linger and suffer for very long." (The conversation the ICU nurse had with me certainly wouldn't fit everyone's situation, but what she said really helped to comfort my aching heart.)

When I flew home to Atlanta the next day, a voicemail awaited me. Louise Walters was practically yelling her message: "Please call! Please call as soon as you can! I don't know where you are, but please call!" I hadn't talked to her in a year, and she would have had no idea that Bernie had been ill. When I reached her, I said, "Louise, I was going to call you as soon as I could. I have sad news. Bernie died yesterday afternoon."

She could barely put words together but managed to recount what had happened two nights before. The Lord had awakened her from a sound sleep with these words: "Bernie Reamer is in terrible pain. He is dying. Pray for the pain." She ignored this prompting as she was still half-asleep. Then the Lord woke her again. He gave her the same information. So she stayed up and began praying for Bernie. Louise's very specific report was comforting, reassuring me it was truly the Lord's timing for taking Bernie. God had spoken to one of my friends to let her know what I already knew.

Her message brought to my remembrance what my friend told me when Bernie was sentenced to prison: *It's real; it's different; but it's not bad.* I applied it to the "now" by telling myself, *My husband is really gone; my life will never be the same, but it's not bad, because God is good.* The wonder of being forewarned seven months beforehand has helped me time and time again with regard to losing Bernie. It has kept me from second-guessing.

In the *Complete Jewish Bible*, God spoke words that I love reflecting on.

"Before I formed you in the womb, I knew you"
(Jeremiah 1:5).

"Your eyes could see me as an embryo, but in
your book all my days were already written; my
days had been shaped before any of them existed"
(Psalm 139:16).

I was learning, more than ever, to say, "Not my will, but yours, Lord." Bernie was God's creation to do with as he pleased. The Lord could have healed him; but I trust in whatever reason he had for taking Bernie away. It's okay.

Yes, there are many unanswered questions concerning Bernie's imprisonment and painful death—but they pale in significance to the reality of God's love, provision, guidance, forgiveness, and—my, oh, my—the spiritual gifts, signs, and *wonders*. There is mystery when it comes to God. The Bible says:

"The secret things belong to the Lord our God,
but the things [that are] revealed belong to us and
to our children forever, that we may follow all the
words of [the commandments]"
(Deuteronomy 29:29 KJV).

I decided to live with that . . . with the mystery. Not for anything in the world, would I return to the life I once lived when I was my own God. I came to him as a spiritual pauper, and now there is richness of soul. I often fail, but there is forgiveness, peace, hope, and security that only God can give.

CHAPTER 28

BREAKING THROUGH PSYCHOSIS

Four months after Bernie died, and finally able to sleep through the night, my life was uprooted once again. A hospital in Del Ray Beach, Florida, called to tell me that my mother and step father were admitted together. I flew down right away thinking, "I'm not up to this, God." But as usual, I found myself up to it because of God's grace—his empowering presence within, to face whatever situation I encountered without.

Just hours after my arrival, my stepfather passed away in ICU from diabetic complications. I must tell my mother . . .

I went to her room and relayed the news. Instead of an appropriate response, my petite mom pulled me close to her and in a low voice encouraged me with, "Judy, you'll never need to worry about financial matters ever again. Eric will pay for everything, including Daddy's funeral."

"Mother dear, who is Eric?"

"He owns the Mitsubishi Auto Corporation and is planning to marry me. Eric's also in the process of buying leer jets for you and all the children."

Suffice it to say that, for the next seven years until her passing, I would need a double dose of grace. Little did I know the journey with my mom would include mental asylums, hospitals, rehabilitation centers, assisted living residences and finally a nursing home. It was the worst of times. Formerly very beautiful, admired, and bright, the latter years had seen Mom robbed of her mind, of her mental acuity.

One day, I received word Mom was being transferred from the hospital to a rehab facility for care. I found myself fearing her imminent death. She refused to move from Florida to Atlanta, so I traveled back and forth. Was there someone at the rehab center who would be willing to talk to Mom about end of life issues, about meeting her Maker? Could someone actually convey any spiritual truth to a woman afflicted with bi-polar disorder and possible schizophrenia?

Her disdain for Jesus Christ had been strong. It's reminiscent of what Daniel, the biblical prophet, wrote about King Nebuchadnezzar—a God-defying, self-exalting king. Nebuchadnezzar's pride caused him to lose everything. The king was reduced to an animal state and went insane. In that debilitated state, God was able to impact him with truth. It's quite a miraculous story where we read of God being powerful enough to break through a darkly-clouded mind.

I made the call to the rehab center, and was connected to her wing.

"Hello. Seventh floor nursing station."

"My mother Rena is in a room on your floor. I'm afraid she may not have long to live. I've a question to ask that might seem strange and rather personal. Do you believe you are going to heaven?"

"I would like to think so. How can anyone be really sure?"

For me, the nurse's response wasn't enough assurance that she'd be the right one to talk to my mother.

"Let me ask you another question, please. Is there anyone on the floor who talks about Jesus?"

"Yes, there is. In fact she is standing right next to me. Would you like to speak with her?"

"Yes! Thank you."

The nurse put the woman next to her on the phone. I repeated, "My mother is on your floor. She may be dying. And . . . have you accepted Jesus as the Messiah?"

"Yes!"

"Do you like to talk about him?"

"I'd rather do that than anything else in the world!"

"You would? What do you do on the wing?"

"I am the social worker."

"Would you present the Gospel regarding Jesus to my mother since I don't know how much longer she has? She will resist you, because she was raised, as I was, to refuse the Gospel . . . and in addition, she is mentally ill. Very. For thirty years Mom has forbidden me to mention Jesus. She won't even let me speak of God or prayer. My mom told me she will never see me again if I bring this up in any way. I have obeyed for many years. But, something is compelling me to make the request of you at this time."

Collette, the social worker, answered, "Let's pray before I go down to see her." I listened as she prayed, "Father, prepare Rena's heart; prepare her for the Gospel. *Quiet her mind.*" The two of us prayed for a few minutes. After hanging up the phone, I lay down on the floor, beseeching God, and waited for the phone to ring. Eventually, the phone rang—Collette.

"When I walked into your mother's room, she was sitting on the edge of her bed. My intention was to make small talk—to break the ice. How would I handle speaking with somebody who I knew was mentally ill? Before I could even get a word out, Rena turned to me, and greeted me with, 'Have you come to talk to me about God and Jesus?'

"I was thrown! Astounded! I told her I had, and asked her if she would like me to do that. Your mother answered, 'Yes, I would'. She was *sane, clear-minded, and alert as ever.* She gave me her full attention. *This wasn't the same Rena I had seen before—or the one the medical records describe. Your mother was in a totally normal frame of mind.* I shared some of the more than three hundred Old Testament prophecies that could only point to one person—Jesus.

"Your mother replied with no resistance other than, 'But, I'm Jewish.' I answered: That's wonderful! Jesus Himself was! I shared with her that the foundation of Christianity is Judaism. She was surprised and accepting of this truth; her mind was sharp; she clearly understood. After we talked for a while, I asked if she'd like to know for sure that she was ready to meet her Maker, her Creator, and to receive his forgiveness. 'Yes.' Then I asked if she believed Jesus to be the long awaited Messiah who was sent by God for the salvation of his people? 'Yes.'

"So I entered into a time of prayer with her and by the time I left the room, Rena was blessed with God's salvation! This was truly miraculous; I knew I hadn't pushed or tried to persuade her. Rena was totally in her right mind the entire visit, and was receptive. Your dear mom and I held hands and prayed as she accepted the Messiah. God had prepared her heart and *quieted her mind.*" Collette related she had walked down the hall and found a Bible to take to a smiling and peaceful Rena.

This was nothing less than answered prayer. Actually supernatural!

There's a biological fact that brought me to a startling realization. The nervous system is a *physical* entity that chemically triggers the responses in the brain. So, what we call "the mind" has physical connections to the body. The manifestation of insanity seen by my mother's psychiatrist was not her soul condition. *God healed her soul of a sickness far worse than any in the body, in her mind.* Sadly for me as her daughter, my mother shortly returned to her mentally altered state after her soul-changing experience.

Is the Lord powerful enough to cure "brains/minds" permanently? Yes, but just as anyone who loves God first and foremost may still have varying degrees of physical problems, so it was with my mother. Her soul had been rescued from spiritual death, though her mind (a physical entity) was still sick. God had temporarily restored her sanity for his purposes. Who knows how long Mom was in her right mind before Collette walked into the room? The miracle for my dear mother was done in *God's* timing, and for the length of time *he* wanted. God planted Collette on Rena's wing, right by the phone when I called. The Lord prompted me as her daughter to call at that exact moment.

My inimitable mom died a few years later, with her soul intact. I couldn't ask for anything more.

> "For what shall it profit a man, if he shall gain the
> whole world, and lose his own soul? (KJV).

CHAPTER 29

STOPPING TO SMELL THE TULIPS

After my mother died, I sat me down, sighed me some good sighs, paced me around the room, sat me down again and sighed me some more sighs. For days, sighing became my new language. I finally faced my latest eyebrow-raising *new* norm. I told myself, Bernie and my mother are just in the next room, albeit a heavenly one.

The new norm actually had its beginnings the night I read Pat Boone's book. The *old* norm had worldly success written all over it. All the "fixins" were in place for success from the time I started grade school in Philadelphia. But God had a fix to fix what I was fixin' to fall into—a life without a heavenly Father.

As a budding artist in my teens, I never could have envisioned creating a painting of my future as it is now. If I'd taken a guess, a sketch illustrating a "happily ever after" scenario would have been a reasonable draft. That's what everyone else pictured for me. Life was seemingly on that track from the time I was little. Everything I touched turned to gold. A glimmering, charming, easy-to-look-at *work of art* was in the making.

"To be or not to be," wrote Shakespeare. My happily-ever-after-life was not to be. Who could have imagined my father would disown me, the rest of the family would be angry and hurtful, and some close friends would reject me? Who could have imagined the loss of worldly goods and reputation, the visits to prison, the death of a fairly young husband, and all those years of my mother's horrendous mental condition?

All I can tell you is, this artist found it challenging to convey her life story in words. If the terms *unexpected, upending, and numbing* were colors, those would be the primary paints on my palette. Then, out of nowhere came a recollection. It was of a powerful word picture. The story was artful, capturing well my feelings. Yes! What the writer sensitively penned would aptly portray the "word" mural I wanted to paint. I thought, *How big is God to have dropped Emily Perl Kingsley's story onto my palette. Her illustration is rich, thick with color and meaning.* Her thoughts have been helpful to untold numbers of people.

Emily and I have corresponded, and were surprised by an interesting connection. My classmate at the University of Maryland, Jim Henson, was a close colleague of Em's (her nickname); they worked closely together for several decades on the most widely watched TV show in the world, with 235 million viewers. To draw Em and me even a few degrees closer: We both lost our husbands of many years to pancreatic cancer.

Here is the article exactly as she wrote it many years ago—

I am often asked to describe the experience of raising a child with a disability—to try to help people who have not shared that unique experience to understand it, to imagine how it would feel. It's like this . . .

When you're going to have a baby, it's like planning a fabulous vacation trip—to Italy. You buy a bunch of guide books and make your wonderful plans. The Coliseum. Michelangelo's David. The gondolas in Venice. You may learn some handy phrases in Italian. It's all very exciting.

After months of eager anticipation, the day finally arrives. You pack your bags and off you go. Several hours later, the plane lands. The flight attendant comes in and says, "Welcome to Holland."

"Holland?!?" you say. "What do you mean Holland?? I signed up for Italy! I'm supposed to be in Italy. All my life I've dreamed of going to Italy."

But there's been a change in the flight plan. They've landed in Holland and there you must stay. The important thing is that they haven't taken you to a horrible, disgusting, filthy place, full of pestilence, famine and disease. It's just a different place. So you must go out and buy new guide books. And you must learn a whole new language. And you will meet a whole new group of people you would never have met.

It's just a different place. It's slower-paced than Italy, less flashy than Italy. But after you've been there for a while and you catch your breath, you look around . . . and you begin to notice that Holland has windmills . . . and Holland has tulips. Holland even has Rembrandts.

But everyone you know is busy coming and going from Italy . . . and they're all bragging about what a wonderful time they had there. And for the rest of your life, you will say "Yes, that's where I was supposed to go. That's what I had planned."

And the pain of that will never, ever, ever, ever go away . . . because the loss of that dream is a very, very significant loss.

But . . . if you spend your life mourning the fact that you didn't get to Italy, you may never be free to enjoy the very special, the very lovely things . . . about Holland.

One of my favorite scriptures supports Emily's (and my) story:

"Do not boast about tomorrow, for you do not know what a day may bring" (Proverbs 27:1).

So welcome to my Holland . . . as I now know it. The tulips are fresh smelling and bright yellow (my favorite color). The dramatic intensity, along with the harmony of light and shadow in the Rembrandt paintings are more wondrous than I ever could have imagined. The serene beauty of windmills astonish me with the power they generate. I could go on and on . . .

And there's one other thing about "Holland"—in fact, it's the main thing. I found God was there. I no longer need to stop and smell the roses, since I'm content to "tiptoe through the tulips." When I gaze at my life's mural, created by Jesus Christ, the greatest living artist, I see a masterpiece.

CHAPTER 30

COMING FULL CIRCLE

Life is hugely interesting at times, isn't it? Not to mention funny and mind boggling. My spiritual adventure started with Pat Boone, and a recent incident brought my journey full circle.

It all began with an invitation to be the speaker at a retreat in Escondido, California. As one who does a lot of traveling, I've grown to love my time at airports and on airplanes. By the time I've left home, my teachings are ready and I can't yet be concerned about details of the conference until I meet the committee. For that reason, being in airports and planes is as relaxing as a spa. I always treat myself to a Nathan's hot dog (I *relish* the thought) and bring along one of the many books friends have suggested I read. I'm a happy camper—that is to say, I'm a happy flier and always feel a little disappointed when the wheels hit the tarmac.

As much as I usually love long flights, on this particular day I was actually excited about disembarking. It was going to be a fun day. Pat Boone, knowing I would be speaking on the West Coast, suggested I come early so we could visit, as we've done several times in the past. He had called a limo company to pick me up at LAX to bring me to his Beverly Hills home.

The fun began with seeing a sign that read "JUDY REAMER," held high by a tall, attractive man—in a chauffeur's uniform, no less. As he graciously seated me in the back of his limo with water and magazines, I looked forward to continuing the relaxation I enjoyed on the plane. I would have preferred a glass partition but figured the driver, Lawrence, wouldn't mind me simply sitting in silence.

It wasn't long before I was lost in thought. Pre-Pat Boone, Judy Reamer was strictly a wife and mother who enjoyed staying home and organizing cabinets, drawers, and closets. I thought about who I was in the past—a virtual nobody outside of my close circle of friends and family. And now I'm a busy inspirational speaker here and abroad, as well as an author, who does guest appearances on TV and radio. I preferred a private arena, but God had another plan for my life.

My reflecting stopped when I noticed the horrendous traffic on Southern California's infamous I-405 expressway. Mild fear befell me when the driver appeared uncertain as to which exit he should take. An uncertainty like this is dangerous on any multi-laned expressway, but in Los Angeles—"Let me outta this limo!"

"Excuse me, sir, but do you know where you are going? You have an address, right?"

That was a ridiculous question for me to ask—and one that could have insulted the man. Now in hindsight—here we go again—*how big is God* to have me ask such a silly thing!

"Yes, I have an address."

"Do you know whose house it is?"

Now why would that matter? As long as he knows the address, it doesn't matter who lives there. Keep quiet, girl, and leave the driving to Lawrence.

"No, I don't know who lives there."

"It's Pat Boone's house."

"I know who Pat Boone is. How do you know him?"

Oh, no! The story is so long, and I want to return to my restful reverie. I'll give him a one-sentence answer, and then I'll go back into my thought cave.

"Pat Boone helped me to know the reality of God."

Now zip your lips, Judy. So many strangers have zipped their lips and stopped up their ears when I've said anything resembling the answer I just gave Lawrence. Certainly this would be the case now.

"Would you repeat that, please?"

"Pat Boone made it possible for me to know that God is very much alive."

"Did you say 'God'?"

"Yes."

At that point, Lawrence leaned forward and laid his head down for a moment on the steering wheel. I thought, *We're going to crash!*

Lawrence lifted his head and said, "I've never had a client ever mention God. You have no idea how amazing it is that you used the word 'God.'"

"Why is that?"

"Just one hour before getting to work, I cried out to a God who I'm not sure exists or would even listen to me if he does. I told him I was a mess. I've done some bad things, but I want to be good. I have no purpose and am lost. I don't know what to do. Nothing is working out in my life. I pleaded with God to give me some sign that he is real and that he heard me. And here you are telling me you know that God is real! Tell me about him!"

Oy Vey! Okay God, we are driving in terrible traffic; I was so looking forward to solitude. There's so much that needs to be shared, but we will soon be arriving at the destination. Even worse, I can't even see Lawrence's face while covering the most important subject in the world!

In a minute, my disquiet ceased, and I felt great excitement to be with this driver who was baring his soul. His words echoed mine from a few decades back. I could relate to his bewilderment and thought of C. S Lewis's words: "No one knows how bad he is until he has tried very hard to be good."

Out of me flowed the account of my own personal journey. Lawrence was so engaged in the story that he got lost twice in Beverly Hills—and not just a slight wrong turn or two; he actually had no idea where he was. In a way, this was fortunate, as it afforded me extra time to share. By now, I had forgotten the excitement of getting to visit with Pat and Shirley. Lawrence and I were in a "dressing room" of sorts, something like that evening when Pat and I were hidden away behind the stage, but instead of Las Vegas, we were now in Beverly Hills. Lawrence asked questions; I gave answers. I became Pat Boone, and this limo driver unwittingly took the part of one Judy Reamer.

Finally, the sleek black vehicle pulled up to the gate, which encompassed Pat's traditional two-storied home. Lawrence came around to open my door at the same time Pat walked out to welcome me with a hug.

I introduced the two men. By now I was looking forward to visiting with Pat but was torn for several reasons. First of all, the conversation with Lawrence was not nearly over. Second, as much as I wanted to stay with the two men, I knew Shirley was waiting inside for Pat and me. What to do? What to say? Should I shove Pat back into the house or shove Lawrence back into his limo?

"Lawrence," I asked, "may I have your phone number?" He wrote it down and handed it to me. We hugged goodbye. Pat looked puzzled by this unusual gesture between limo driver and passenger. *Had Judy and Lawrence been neighbors or found out they were third cousins or something?*

Lawrence drove off as Pat and I came through the front door. We walked straight into the sitting room where Shirley was seated—the room where Bible studies were held for the rich and famous—household names around the world. The Boones had taken care of many "Judys" right in their home.

Pat smilingly asked me, "What was all that about with the limo driver?"

"Oh, Pat, it was a glorious ride." I gave him all the details and added how much the man resembled the Judy of the past.

"We should have invited him in," Pat said. "I didn't know all that was happening. You can give him a call sometime."

"No, Pat, I'm not comfortable doing that since we're both single and . . . well, you know."

"Then may I have his number, Judy?"

Two weeks later this email came from Shirley:

> Hi Judy,
>
> We met with your driver, Lawrence. He's a sweetheart! Pat invited him over to the house, but on the day he was to visit, his car died—and he had lost his job—so Pat drove all the way to pick him up.
>
> Lawrence talked openly and we did the same. He accepted Jesus as his Savior. Pat baptized him in our pool. We sent him home with a Bible and both our books. Praising the Lord for His great

providence in having you as a passenger! We stay
in touch with him.

Love always,
Shirley

Lawrence's life was changed. Decades earlier, mine was too. What's interesting is that God's still working through my Hollywood teenage idol . . . in the same way. Pat is exemplary in his willingness to stop along the way to help someone in need—even though, from what I know about this still-handsome performer, he is one of the busiest men in the world.

We've come full circle. Because of Pat, I was helped and was then able to help Lawrence. Pat had the pleasure of participating in the "sealing" of what had started in the limo.

Pat's book has also come full circle with *this* book. If anyone's life is changed as a result of this story, I'd have to point with thanks to Pat Boone, who would, as always, point with thanks to God—what a WONDER!

RESOURCES

MEETING GOD FOR YOURSELF . . . IF YOU HAVEN'T ALREADY

There's only one reason to read this section—and that is, you want what happened to me *to happen to you*. Just as I wanted what happened to Pat Boone to happen to me. And what was that? A new beginning. A fresh start. A cleansing. A rebirth.

There is a major truth indelibly written on my heart and mind. Here's what I remind myself of daily: God's priority is not to make me happy. Please don't misunderstand: Often there *is* elation, but the Lord's main desire is to make me holy. This fact explains much of what I've experienced over the years. Happiness and perfect relationships await me in heaven. As long as I am on the earth, the Lord is ever at work so my life may increase in godliness and decrease in old selfish habits, coping mechanisms, and wrong responses. He's training me to be fully dependent on him, rather than to live independently and use him only if I start to feel unhappy.

The truth is, whether the worship of God becomes central in a life or not, varying amounts of trials and suffering will continue. The Bible is very clear that "in this world you will have trouble," and my story is a good illustration, as I had more than a few difficulties after my "mountaintop experience" in Las Vegas. But I can attest to another biblical truth—that those who lean on God have a gigantic advantage over those who continue to live for themselves. Dependence only upon God affords me the gift of peace in the midst of storms—a priceless benefit. Just as peace *with* God cannot be bought, neither can the peace *of* God.

Throughout the story, it's amazing how the Lord made sure I was at the right place at the right time with the right people—or with the right book (Pat Boone's). My son Johnny spoke these wise words: "In order to realize how big God is, we need to first realize how small we are."

Early on in my seeking I did not have an answer for "Is there life after death?" Maybe you've asked this question before. I now trust we will never die—that is, the soul lives forever, though the body will die. The historical documents written by the biblical authors draw attention to this over and over. So if the soul lives forever, the question is, "Where?"

To find the answer, consider these facts.

Fact 1: God Is Loving

Where would one go to find whether this is true? The entire Bible announces his love! Here are two verses out of multitudes that attest to this certainty.

From the Old Testament:

> "The Lord appeared to us in the past, saying: 'I have loved you with an everlasting love; I have drawn you with unfailing kindness'"(Jeremiah 31:3).

From the New Testament:

> "And hope does not put us to shame, because God's love has been poured out into our hearts through the Holy Spirit, who has been given to us" (Romans 5:5).

Fact 2: Humans Sin

Adam and Eve really had it easy before they sinned. They didn't have to figure out for themselves what was good and what was bad. All the couple had to do was depend on God for everything. Sadly, they didn't recognize the perfect love, provision, and power of the God who was taking care of them.

So they traded a life of walking and talking with God for a life of independent living. That is the ultimate root of sin—independence from the Creator. Adam and Eve were now in charge of determining right from wrong. Once they chose to listen to the fallen angel Satan (a.k.a. Lucifer), they were expelled from the Garden of Eden, a heaven on earth.

From now on, the first man and woman had no one to look to but themselves. I wonder if they began mulling, *I used to be someone special, a person of worth. I vaguely recall something like that in my past. But right now I don't know who I am, what I am here for, or what I am to do.*

Confusion reigned in Adam and Eve, later becoming the norm for all of mankind. Within the soul of every human being, there is a distant sense of lost significance and adequacy. No one can recapture it, no matter how diligent he is. You've read my story; that was precisely my frustration.

Fact 3: God's View of Sin

For many, the reality of their sin never burdens them. They see sin as little more than a misfortune, a weakness, a failing, or some kind of maladjustment. This is not God's perspective.

The Bible is where to look for the Lord's viewpoint. God did not simply sit back and tolerate disobedience to his directives; the book of Leviticus describes the sacrifices required as payment for sin. Without reading Scripture, one might wonder if God is intolerant. Through reading the Bible, however, I came to an understanding that caused me to agree with God's demands for holiness, purity, faithfulness, and obedience.

I have totally embraced Psalm 111:10:

> "The fear of the LORD is the beginning of wisdom; all who follow his precepts have good understanding."

God meant what he said, with good reason. The following two verses contain descriptions of God's righteous indignation:

> "Dearly beloved, avenge not yourselves, but rather give place unto wrath: for it is written, 'Vengeance is mine; I will repay saith the Lord'" (Romans 12:19).

> "God is just: He will pay back trouble to those who trouble you and give relief to you who are troubled, and to us as well. This will happen when the Lord Jesus is revealed from heaven in blazing fire with his powerful angels. He will punish those who do not know God and do not obey the gospel of our Lord Jesus. They will be punished

with everlasting destruction and shut out from
the presence of the Lord and from the glory of his
might" (2 Thessalonians 1:6-9).

It's only fair that people who have wronged us must answer to God—either here on earth or after they die—for the hurt they caused. The same applies to me. Sin demands compensation. Only the truly contrite heart qualifies for his mercy. What if a person refuses to accept Jesus as Savior, thereby cutting himself off from the forgiveness God offers? There will be hell to pay. I believe this verse:

"And the smoke of their torment will rise for
ever and ever. There will be no rest day or night"
(Revelation 14:11).

And that's the answer to my original question which was: *So if the soul lives forever, the question is, Where?* One of two places.

Although God is just in meting out retribution, he is abundantly merciful. So now let's consider forgiveness that comes from God. What does it look like? Well, when God forgives sin—my sin, your sin—it is obliterated. Gone. There is no payback.

The meaning of the word *gospel* is "good news." And it just doesn't get any better than this! I love the taste, the sound, the feel of God's forgiveness. To make an analogy, here are some of my favorite things: Florence, Italy; snowstorms; spaghetti; classical ballet; comfortable shoes; good books; close friends. But these don't hold a candle to being forgiven by God. Imagine! Shame, guilt, and distress are replaced with rest and relief. Redemption, acceptance, love, joy, peace, comfort, guidance, friendship, and forgiveness are all included when we accept Jesus as Lord of our life.

Fact 4: God Is Sovereign

Theologian and author Dr. Harry Ironside (1876-1951) told about a man who described how God had sought him and found him, loved him, called him, saved him, delivered him, cleansed him, and healed him. It was a tremendous testimony to the glory of God. After the meeting, one Christian took the man aside and said, "You know, I appreciate all that you said about what God did for you, but you did not mention anything about your part in it. Salvation is really part us and part God, and you should have mentioned something about your part."

"Oh," the man replied, "I apologize. I am sorry. I really should have mentioned that my part was running away, and God's part was running after me until I found Him."

Ironside's story illustrates God's sovereignty, which the following verses underscore:

> "All the peoples of the earth are regarded as nothing. He does as he pleases with the powers of heaven and the peoples of the earth. No one can hold back his hand or say to him: 'What have you done?'" (Daniel 4:35).

> "There is no wisdom, no insight, no plan that can succeed against the LORD" (Proverbs 21:30).

Fact 5: The Messiah Came to Bear Our Sin—Past and Future.

Sin created a separation between Creator and his creation. But our loving God, desiring communion with mankind, set in motion a redemptive plan.

"By this gospel you are saved, if you hold firmly to the word I preached to you. Otherwise, you have believed in vain. For what I received I passed on to you as of first importance: that Christ died for our sins according to the Scriptures" (1 Corinthians 15:2-3).

Fact 6: A New Way of Living Begins

When we place trust in Jesus, God becomes our life. Jesus gave his life *to* us, in order to live *in* us, in order to live *through* us.

"On that day you will realize that I am in my Father, and you are in me, and I am in you" (John 14:20).

Once we acknowledge this truth, we will be able to live by the wisdom of Proverbs 3:5, 6:

"Trust in the LORD with all your heart and lean not on your own understanding; in all your ways submit to him, and he will make your paths straight."

This new way of living enables us to give an enthusiastic confirmation to what Jesus promised:

"I came that they may have life and have it abundantly" (John 10:10).

What Does It Mean to Believe?

What turns mere believing into redeeming faith? At its core, salvation has two parts. When these work together, a supernatural transformation occurs. "The Christian life means living in the *two halves* of reality: the supernatural and the natural parts." (Francis A. Schaeffer, *True Spirituality*)

Both elements were present in my story. One part was the intellectual acceptance that there is a God who rules the universe; the other part was the realization that this God spoke *"Let there be light"* over me. Without that amazing "touch" of the Lord, which caused my heart to sing a new song, there wouldn't have been a transformation.

John Piper, author of *Future Grace* wrote, "Being persuaded that Jesus and his promises are factual is not by itself saving faith. That is why some professing Christians will be shocked at the last day, when they hear him [Jesus] say, 'I never knew you,' even though they protest that he is 'Lord, Lord.'"

Liken this to seeing a spectacular movie that caused you to laugh and cry. Yet on exiting the theater, you have no intention of applying the movie's message to your life. In fact, you leave wondering where the nearest coffee house is, and that's it—no more.

Similarly, it may be true that you thoroughly enjoyed my book and intend to suggest it to others, but you have no intention of embracing God or making him central in your daily life.

On the other hand, as you read *to him* from the pages of *your* life, it's going to be a unique conversation. There is nobody just like you. Your vocabulary or grammar won't really matter when you're chatting with God. This isn't about how you present yourself. Whether you stammer or speak eloquently is immaterial. It's about developing an authentic friendship, without pretense.

If you were measuring behavior on a scale of one to ten, with ten being the worst, where would you place yourself with regard to word and deed? You may be off the charts as far as "badness" goes. Just know there is nothing you are doing, thinking, or saying that will shock God. He is unshakable! *And* he already knows your sins.

On the other hand, you may be giving yourself a score of "four" since you feel you have far fewer failings than the average person. However, you need to be "born again" just as much as a slanderer or a vicious dictator. There is no one in the entire world who does not need to be spiritually recreated.

Since you will be conversing with a holy, glorious, loving, perfect God, you'll probably experience an internalized conviction of sin—a sense of uncleanness. Let the Lord know you recognize specific ways you have wronged him. Have you mistreated others, behaved miserably, thought badly? Painful emotions may rise up as you express yourself: You may think, *Woe is me!* That's godly sorrow—a great thing in God's sight. Forgiveness stands at the door, so receive it as the best gift in your life! Oh, to stand before the Lord blameless! And that's what acknowledging your sins before him will afford you. Shame and condemnation get washed away by a holy God when one admits there is depravity within the heart. Discover the joy of a clear conscience!

You might wonder why people continue to sin even after the initial transformation—the *new birth*. Well, it takes time to get used to the new "heart" God placed inside of us. If we sin, that doesn't mean the transformation is undone.

The old habit patterns in behavior, thought, and speech developed strong muscles over the years when we were our own God. Biblically, the name for these strong muscles is "the flesh." Every child of God will die with inadequacies, but if we yearn to mature in our faith, little by little there will be a lessening of the self-centeredness that once plagued us. Why? Because the Holy Spirit will be working inside us to effect nothing less than amazing changes of attitude and actions.

By his grace we were born anew, and by that same grace, we will increase in godliness. *What is grace?* It is the empowering presence of God, which enables us to be all that God created us to be and enables us to do all that God created us to do. And yes, it can also point to his undeserved mercy!

> "So I say, walk by the Spirit, and you will not gratify the desires of the flesh" (Galatians 5:16).

What I've written in this section has been my story, my song. God met me where I was. According to every individual's "chart," the Lord determines how to guide, comfort, encourage, strengthen, and deliver.

I can think of no better way to end this section than by passing on a message from God to you: He's saying, *"Talk to Me!"*

RESOURCES: FOR THE JEWISH READER

PART 1 AND PART 2

PART 1: JUDAISM 101— AN INTRIGUING HISTORY

Jewish people typically have one of two reactions when they encounter someone who believes the New Testament is the completion of the Jewish Scriptures. One reaction is, "I want to hear your story, but don't quote me the Bible." The other is, "I'm not interested in your experience; just quote me the Bible."

In one short week I reacted both ways. Pat Boone told of his experience in his book, which provoked me to jealousy. I wanted what he *experienced*.

On the other side of the coin were the Bible proofs, which Pat explained for hours after his show in Las Vegas. Pulling an all-nighter in college produced high grades, but pulling an all-nighter in Pat's dressing room produced a working knowledge of the Scriptures. Isn't it interesting that the Old Testament Scriptures themselves were the best and most thorough source available to help me understand the identity of Jesus? And God used a Hollywood icon who knew where to turn.

All that has happened to me grew out of my own heritage and my own personal story. Seeing the whole picture caused me to be excited about my Jewish Scriptures and the majestic, beautiful history that led up to the wonderful gift God gave to the world. This great salvation was the missing puzzle piece that opened my eyes and ears, delivering me from years of being a "wondering Jew."

Sadly, I knew so little about my Jewish past. Maybe the following short history will enlarge your knowledge of your heritage.

Beginnings

Judaism began approximately 4,000 years ago. The Jewish people, also known as "Hebrews" trace their ancestry to "Eber," the traditional forefather of the Hebrew people mentioned in Genesis 10:21 "Unto Shem also, the father of all the children of Eber, the elder brother of Jepheth even to him *were children* born."

This same verse of the Old Testament mentions Shem, one of Noah's three sons. From this name, the word "Semitic" has entered our vocabulary, describing both the Jewish and Arabic people.

Abraham

Jews believe that God called a descendant of Eber named Abram to leave his family and the adulterous people of Ur of the Chaldees and go to the land of Canaan:

> "Now the Lord had said unto Abram, 'Get thee out
> of thy country, and from thy kindred, and from
> thy father's house, unto a land that I was shew

thee: And I will make a of thee a great nation, and
I will bless thee, and make thy name great; and
thou shall be a blessing: And I will bless them that
bless thee, and curse him that curseth thee: and
in thee shall all families of the earth be blessed'"
(Genesis 12:1-3).

This promise to Abram (whose name God later changed to Abraham), was also repeated to Abraham's son, Isaac, and his grandson Jacob (who was later renamed, Israel). The descendants of Israel (the Jewish people) repeatedly pointed to God's early communication with their forefathers as proof that they were God's Chosen People. They continued to see themselves in this way, even when Jacob later moved his family to Egypt to escape a severe famine and they found themselves enslaved to the Egyptians.

Moses

During this time, they cried out for a Deliverer, and God finally sent Moses to deliver them from the hand of Pharaoh. Moses led the children out of Egypt by the power of God, and this deliverance became the foundation of the Jewish belief in a God who cared deeply for them as His Children and freed them from their bondage. Following their liberation, God gave Moses the Law (including the Ten Commandments). God's communication with Moses during this time became the foundation for early Jewish Scripture; Moses is the author of the Torah, the first five books of the Jewish Canon, recording the early history of the Jewish people and the Law given by God.

The Promised Land

After Moses died, Joshua took over the leadership and the Jews entered the Promise Land. They had to conquer many inhabitants. After Joshua died, the nation of Israel was governed by judges for 350 years. During the time of the Judges, the Israelites wanted to be led by a king. God eventually provided this king, even though it was not what he wanted for his People. Saul took the throne as the first King of Israel, and after he nearly destroyed the nation, David became the second King, conquering the city of Jerusalem and establishing it as Israel's capital.

After David died, his son, Solomon, became the third King. He built a temple to the Lord, and Israel thrived under his leadership. During this time, prophets rose in the nation of Israel and began to have an impact on the culture and theology of the Jews. Amos, for example, urged the Israelites to develop a personal and national obedience to God; Hosea described God as a source of mercy and love; Isaiah highlighted God's majesty and righteousness; Micah called the Jews to "do justly, and to love kindness and to walk humbly with thy God."

Divided Kingdoms

After the reign of King Solomon, the nation was divided into two smaller kingdoms—the southern kingdom known as Judea (with Jerusalem as its capital) and the northern kingdom (with Samaria as its capital). Both the Northern and Southern kingdoms were continually at war with other nations until both were conquered. The Syrians conquered the Northern Kingdom in 721 B.C.E. and the Babylonians conquered the Southern Kingdom in 606 B.C.E. The Jews found themselves in captivity once again. During this time, the prophet Ezekiel provided a glimmer of hope by encouraging the Jews to worship God in Babylon just as they had in Jerusalem. He cast a vision of a new Jewish nation that would come in the future and reminded the Jews of God's promises to their forefathers. Those Jews who were not in captivity were dispersed among the nations of the world. It was during this time that the institution of the synagogue developed alongside the office of the Rabbi.

Return to Jerusalem

When the Persians captured Babylon in 538 B.C.E. many Jews were allowed to return and rebuild Jerusalem under the leadership of Ezra. It was during this time that the reading of the Torah and other Scriptures became very important. The second temple was built in 520 B.C.E. A Priestly code was developed and formal, legalistic Judaism emerged in this new period of history. Jewish independence was not long-lasting, however.

Destruction of the Temple

The Roman Empire made Israel a state of Rome in 63 B.C.E. In response to Jewish rebellion, Titus (the historic Roman general) eventually destroyed the city of Jerusalem and the Jewish temple in 70 A.D. After the destruction of Jerusalem and the temple, the Jews were once again scattered all over the world. Following the fall of Jerusalem, Hebrew scholars gathered and eventually established the Jewish Canon of Scripture, including the Torah (the Law), The Prophets, and the Writings as we have them today. Later the Mishnah, (commentaries on the law) was compiled as well. As the center of Jewish learning shifted to Babylon, the Gemara (sermonic material that addresses all areas of Jewish life) was also assembled. The Gemara was eventually added to the Mishnah and the combined volume became known as the Talmud. The Torah and the Talmud continue to be recognized as important religious writings that guide the Jewish people.

Today, Judaism continues as one of the oldest of the world's major living religions. In 2015, Judaism reported an estimated 14.2 million Jews throughout the world, concentrated mainly in North America and Israel (approximately 6 million).

How Judaism Answers "What's the nature of the Creator and creation?"

While Judaism is clearly the foundation for Christianity, there are a number of important differences and one of these differences lies in the nature of God. The misconception that the Jewish Scriptures picture a God of wrath, while the New Testament portrays a God of love is not entirely tenable. From the New Testament:

> "But because of your stubbornness and your unrepentant heart, you are storing up wrath against yourself for the day of God's wrath, when his righteous judgment will be revealed" (Romans 2:5).

From the Old Testament:

> "And he passed in front of Moses, proclaiming, 'The LORD, the LORD, the compassionate and gracious God, slow to anger, abounding in love and faithfulness . . . '" (Exodus 34:5,6).

Judaism teaches that there is one universal God; Jews are strict monotheists who view God as a single, indivisible entity (unlike Christians who view God as Trinitarian; a single entity with three personalities, the Father, Son and Holy Spirit). Jews believe that this God has revealed his nature and will through the Jewish Prophets, particularly Abraham and Moses, point to the Messiah. And, Jews also believe that divine revelation is progressive and continues to this day through the scholars and rabbis of Judaism. The religion teaches that humans are the special creation of this God, and that they have been created with special characteristics uncommon to other animals:

> "So God created in his *own* image, in the image
> of God created he him; male and female created
> he them" (Genesis 1:27).

How Judaism Answers the Question:
"How Did It Get So Messed Up?"

So, if people are capable of choosing "good," why is the world such a messed up place? From a Jewish perspective, it's really a matter of choice and behavior. Jews generally consider actions and behavior to be of primary importance. In other words, "beliefs come out of actions." This is very different from the conservative Christian worldview. For Christians, "belief" is of primary importance and "actions" simply flow from beliefs. From the Jewish perspective, the world is messed up because people don't behave as they should. They make wrong choices.

Jews do not accept the Christian concept of original sin (the belief that all people have inherited Adam and Eve's sin when they disobeyed God's instructions in the Garden of Eden). Jews don't see man's fallen nature as the root of the problem because they don't believe that humans have a "nature" problem in the first place! From the Jewish perspective, mankind is inherently free to make the choice for good or evil; each human being has the capacity to be good, kind and obedient to the Laws of God.

How Judaism Answers the Question: "How Do We Fix It?"

Before we delve into how Judaism answers this question, let us look at the foundational principles as given by Rabbi Moshe ben Maimon, (also known as "Maimonides"). He is generally accepted as one of the most important Jewish scholars of medieval times and he listed thirteen principles of faith:

1. *God exists and is the sole Creator.*
2. *God is unique.*
3. *God has no bodily form or shape.*
4. *God is eternal.*
5. *We should pray to God and to Him only.*
6. *The words of the Prophets are true.*
7. *The prophecies of Moses are true and he is the greatest of the Prophets.*
8. *The written Torah and the Talmud are true.*
9. *The Torah is not subject to change.*
10. *God knows the thoughts of every person.*
11. *God will reward those who are good.*
12. *The Messiah will come.*
13. *The dead will be resurrected.*

Now, to address the question—

Well, if the problem is simply a matter of choosing wrong behaviors, then the solution is really quite simple.

It's merely a matter of learning what the "right" behaviors are, and then doing what we have learned we ought to do. In each of these three manifestations of Judaism—Orthodox, Conservative and Reformed—behavior is the focus of religious activity.

Judaism is a faith system that is built on the good works of its adherents. These good works are derived from a number of fundamental beliefs that are accepted by all religious Jews to one degree or another. This is why Jewish believers place such a high priority on doing good works, making sacrifices, and doing good deeds in order to please God. To fix the problem, each sect has its particular approach:

Orthodox Judaism

This is the oldest branch of Judaism. Orthodox Jews try to follow the "letter of the law" by obeying the Torah and the original customs and traditions of the earliest Jews. They look upon every word in the Torah, Mishnah and the Talmud as divinely inspired. They are rigorous about ritual observances, the dietary laws, and keeping the Sabbath.

Reform Judaism

This movement within Judaism started in the 1790s in Germany, and today, Reform Judaism has moved away from the strict observances of the Orthodox branch of the faith. Reform Jews believe that the principles taught in the Scriptures are far more important than the practices. They follow the ethical laws of Judaism, but leave up to the individual the decision whether to follow or ignore the dietary and other traditional laws. They have loosened many of the Old Testament regulations.

Conservative Judaism

This form of Judaism began in the mid-nineteenth century as a reaction to the Reform Movement. Conservative Judaism attempts to find a middle ground between the Orthodox and Reform. Conservatives retain much of the tradition of Judaism while making accommodations for modern lifestyles. As an example, some of the dietary restrictions are not followed, and there's an emphasis on rabbinical commentaries and oral traditions that adapt to the conditions of the modern world. As a result, this sect is less rigid than Orthodox observances.

PART 2: "OKAY, I REALIZE THE WORLD IS MESSED UP, BUT AM I MESSED UP?"

My rabbi taught me I was good, but what do the Scriptures say? As humans, are we basically good or bad? If we are good, maybe we don't need saving. But, if we are basically fallen, incapable of obeying the rules in a way that would satisfy God, a Savior may just be what we need. I had no clue that "Savior" was an Old Testament term used multiple times. My thinking was that the word was exclusive to Christianity, and as a result, I wanted no part of it. Had I been a Bible reader, "Savior" wouldn't have been a stumbling block.

A simple empirical observation of our own lives and the lives of those around us provides us with more than enough evidence to know that people are naturally inclined toward evil. Doesn't this explain why we need to understand that we surely need a power outside of ourselves for redemption? A Redeemer. A Savior. A Messiah.

The Jewish Scriptures below, which most of Jewry have never read, paint a picture that stopped me in my tracks:

> "The heart *is* deceitful above *all* things, and desperately sick: who can know it?" (Jeremiah 17:9).

> "The fool hath said in his heart, There is no God. They are corrupt, they have done abominable works, there is none that doeth good. The Lord looked down from heaven upon the children of men, to see if there were any that did understand, and seek God. They are all gone aside, they are all together become filthy: there is none that doeth good, no, not one" (Psalm 14:1-3).

According to Psalm 14 above, I'm *not* good. If I can't do *anything* to please God, how can I be forgiven? I had formerly believed that if I observed Yom Kippur, my righteousness would be established, albeit just one year at a time. I'd be able to start the Jewish New Year afresh. But old habits, old responses, old emotions would kick in immediately after the Day of Atonement.

I came to realize the Jewish sacrificial system demanded a death.

> "For the life of the flesh is in the blood; and I have given it to you upon the altar to make atonement for your souls: for it is the blood that maketh an atonement for the soul" (Leviticus 17:11).

However, once the Second Temple was destroyed by the Romans in 70 A.D., there was no longer a biblically appropriate place for the Israelites to be forgiven by God through animal sacrifices. Yet the fact that they could no longer sacrifice animals at the Temple did not nullify the necessity of shedding blood for the atonement of sins.

Seven hundred years earlier, the prophet Isaiah spoke to the people, declaring that there would be a Redeemer, a Savior, known as the Holy One of Israel (Isaiah 54:5). It was foretold what this Redeemer would accomplish for unrighteous man:

"He shall bear their iniquities" (Isaiah 53:11).

What do you think is the main reason someone decides to fervently call upon God? Mostly everyone who does so has first tried every other solution to remedy his or her situation. No bootstraps are left. This described my own behavior the night I fell to the floor in tears, unable to read one more page of Pat Boone's book. My sobbing had nothing to do with any desire to please, serve, or get right with God. Surprisingly, this is the common denominator among us. For selfish reasons, we turn to him.

Want to know what my first words to God were? Here's what I said:

"I'm so tired of trying to be good. I take one step forward and two steps backward. The malice I have for my stepparents and the ache of an emotionally distant father—I can't stop the hatred, and it hurts terribly. I'm also smoking some, and it really bothers Bernie. Besides, which, smoking is harmful. I'm beginning to enjoy a second drink and am afraid this will lead to alcohol dependency. And not only that, but I am addicted to TV. At times, I have been greedy, lustful, and selfish. I've caught myself gossiping and feeling jealous. I'm beginning to curse for the first in my life, which shocks me."

I was hopeful there was a God who was listening to me. Pat had written that God would be there for anyone who cried out to him. I had nothing to lose and was miserable with my sin nature. "I'm worn out, God," I went on. "I'm unable to be the person I want to be. And the person I don't want to be, that's who I am."

This praying to an unseen God was wholly for my own benefit. Yet, God met me in my self-centeredness. I had only a small understanding of my need for repentance. "I've been wrong; I've wanted my own way; I've wanted to be my own God" was not at the forefront of my initial conversation with God, though it was there. I was sobbing not so much in godly regret, but rather in self-pity. It wasn't until I came into a relationship with him that I finally understood the necessity of true humility before God in agreeing with him about my walking after the flesh.

Early in my faith walk, it had been that I wanted relief from self-condemnation, personal pain, and the pressure of my own selfish nature. But as the months passed, my attitude changed to: *I've been wrong, God; I have wronged you terribly, ignored you hugely and loved you poorly. If I'm going to amend my ways, I need your grace and power to effect those changes.*

This new outlook was birthed from a soul transformation. I hadn't ever wanted to do wrong, think improperly, or have bad attitudes, but my reasons were different now: I loved this Savior, this Redeemer, this Messiah, because I was experiencing his love for me. Now, my motivation was that I wanted to please *him*.

The Numbers Speak for Themselves

The mathematical probability that one person could fulfill just a few of the messianic prophecies is infinitesimal, yet Jesus did it. To get a feel for the probabilities involved, consider this: Author and speaker Josh McDowell calculated the odds of Jesus fulfilling only *eight* of the messianic prophecies as 1 out of 10¹⁷ (a one followed by seventeen zeros). This is equivalent to covering the entire state of Texas with silver dollars two feet deep, marking one of them, mixing them all up, and having a blind-folded person select the marked one at random the first time.

Here are just a few of the many prophecies that Jesus did fulfill:

The Messiah would come from the tribe of Judah. *Genesis 49:10*
The Messiah would be born of a virgin. *Isaiah 40:3*
The Messiah would appear after the Jews return to Israel. *Jeremiah 23:3-6* \
The Messiah would be born in Bethlehem. *Micah 5:2*
The Messiah would be preceded by a messenger. *Isaiah 40:3*
The Messiah would enter Jerusalem while riding on a donkey. *Zechariah 9:9*
The Messiah would suffer and be rejected. *Isaiah 53:3*
The Messiah would be betrayed for 30 pieces of silver. *Zechariah 11:12-13*
The Messiah would be silent before his accusers. *Isaiah 53:7*
The Messiah would be wounded, whipped, and crucified. *Isaiah 53:5*
The Messiah would suffer at the crucifixion. *Psalm 22:1*
The Messiah would be crucified with criminals. *Psalm 22:19*
The Messiah would be buried in a rich man's tomb. *Isaiah 53:12*

I leave you with the ancient benediction I've heard countless times from childhood to the present—

> **The LORD bless thee, and keep thee: The LORD make his face shine upon thee, and be gracious unto thee: The LORD lift up his countenance upon thee, and give thee peace (Numbers 6:24-26).**

ACKNOWLEDGMENTS

"I not only use all the brains that I have, but all that I can borrow."—Woodrow Wilson

"Many looks have helped this book."—Judy Reamer >grin<

The following were the unique *lookers,* who differed in their God-given assignments to get this book done before it did me in!

Donna Alberta (MI), Karen Barber (GA), Lana Bueno (GA), Wes Clemmer (PA), Sandy Feit (GA), Dave Kopp (NY), Laine and Mike Riley (GA), Janice Scott (GA), Marsha Thorson (CO), Diane Woerner (TN)

Though few of these friends knew each other, they were all part of a team that covered the bases, which included . . .

- Persuading me to write the book when it was the last thing I wanted to do.
- Moving in with for several days to frame the earliest draft.
- Giving immeasurable generous assistance, which was paramount in launching the book.
- Using their keen ideas for details as well as knowing the value of a well-placed comma or em dash.
- Making me laugh when I'd start to whine.
- Enthusiastically encouraging me with, "Judy, you *are* a good writer!"
- Coming alongside during a crisis and working with me in the midst of an awful scare.
- Asking insightful questions that pushed me to dig deeper.

Towards the end of the writing journey, when I wanted to run away to some far-flung spot, my dear friend Sandy Feit, an incomparable copy editor, volunteered to run with me—not to Antarctica, but to the finish line of *Wonder*. This trouper went the distance with me, never letting go of my hand or the book. She kept me focused and sane. "Thank you" is too weak a phrase to use for this fellow (well, female) Jewish believer.

In addition, I am beyond grateful to Emily Perl Kingsley for lending me her powerful article, which gives my story significant closure. ("Welcome to Holland" by Emily Perl Kingsley, ©1987 by Emily Perl Kingsley. All rights reserved. Reprinted by permission of the author.)

I am indebted to J. Warner Wallace, *Cold Case Christianity*, who granted permission to use anything from pleaseconvinceme.com that would enhance the Resources section of the book.

It is no mere coincidence that WestBow Press, a division of Thomas Nelson Publishers and Zondervan, wound up partnering with me. They used their know-how and graciousness to encourage me. I am thankful for all who expertly did their jobs—especially Gwen Ash, who shepherded me through the publishing process.

CPSIA information can be obtained at www.ICGtesting.com
Printed in the USA
LVOW07s2356060515

437499LV00002B/6/P